The Week That Changed the world

The Week That Changed the World

THE COMPLETE EASTER STORY

Timothy Dean Roth

This harmonization of the four gospels is based on *Today's New International Version,* copyright © 2005 by the International Bible Society and used by permission.

Cover image courtesy of iStockphoto
Cover design by Corey Kent
Interior design by Vicki K. Black

           Library of Congress Cataloging-in-Publication Data
Roth, Timothy Dean.
The week that changed the world : the complete Easter story / Timothy Dean Roth.
       p.   cm.
ISBN 978-1-59627-106-7 (pbk.)
1. Holy Week. 2. Easter. I. Title.
BT414.R68 2009
226'.1—dc22
                                            2009017681

Printed in the United States of America.

Seabury Books
445 Fifth Avenue
New York, New York 10016
www.seaburybooks.com
An imprint of Church Publishing Incorporated

5   4   3   2   1

For
Robert E. Webber
1933–2007

Contents

Foreword

A SUBJECT I FREQUENTLY returned to in my Wheaton College classes was the contemporary relevance of the ancient church and its liturgies. "Stop reinventing the wheel!" I would frequently shout.

One of the bright young men that got this message was Tim Roth. Now, Tim comes forth with his own call to return to the sources. Christianity, he cries, is not only a supernatural event, a divine book, it is also God incarnate. If you want to be touched by God incarnate and have your life changed forever, it will only happen when you meet Jesus as the man who did for you what you cannot do for yourself. Everywhere you meet this man, but nowhere do you meet him as in the last days of his life.

Tim weaves the parallel stories of Jesus' final days into an original and brilliant unified text that lifts the ancient story right into your own.

Don't just read it. The story is meant to be prayed, to be made real in the consciousness of your own life. Today this story is real for me as I struggle with the end of my own life due to terminal cancer. Thanks for this story which is more than a story. It's life. Resurrected life! Become it—and be made whole.

— ROBERT E. WEBBER

Acknowledgments

Without the following people, their support and prayers, this book would not have been possible.

Chad and Jane Nicholson, Clark Rivinoja, Melissa and Jacob Florer-Bixler, Joshua Casteel, Joseph and Nora Clair, Matt and Seeca Smalley, Phyllis Roth, Michael Christensen, Gene and Roseann Blankenship, Cynthia Leininger, Robert Leininger, Aaron and Angela, Steve Kunselman, Peggy Christensen, Fr. Matthew O'Leary, Terry Lindvall, Michelle Pruitt, Ellen Davis, Richard Ashcroft, Thea Portier-Young, Bo Bonner, Adam Baron, Jim Roth, Ben Irwin, Bob and Joanne Webber, Helen Umphrey, Doctors Lundy, Knopf, and Edwards, Mary Bodine, Margie Haguewood, Sesilia Tamate, Sarah Swafford, Andy Meisenheimer, Sue Brower, Paul Engle, Stan Gundry, the Committee on Bible Translation and the International Bible Society, Cynthia Shattuck, Vicki Black, and Lucas Smith.

And thank you to all of my family and friends on the sidelines who cheered me on.

✠

The Complete Easter Story

BEGINNING WITH PALM SUNDAY, the gospels record every day of Jesus' life up to the time of his death and resurrection. These eight days are unparalleled in the canon of scripture for their narrative power, detail, and focus. Nowhere else in the Bible do we have such an extended account of a single event, and appropriately so, since these eight days form the central event of the Christian faith. About a third of Jesus' teachings, as recorded in scripture, come from this one week. These eight days, then, commonly called Holy Week, cannot be underestimated for their impact on the history of Christianity and of the world.

This book brings together the four individual gospel accounts of Holy Week and merges them into one seamless narrative, while keeping every detail present in each of the four gospels fully intact. Instead of dividing the story by chapter and verse, this book divides the story into the days on which the events happened, so that you can follow along day by day during Holy Week—reliving, in a sense, the words on the page. Two chapters are added to the beginning to lead us into, and prepare us for, Holy Week, while two final chapters take us from Easter Sunday to Pentecost. The book is subtitled *The Complete Easter Story* because it contains, with these additional four chapters, every detail given in the gospels from December, the Feast of Hanukkah, to the following May and the Day of Pentecost. It is an invitation to spend twelve days with Jesus and his disciples during this season, to experience as fully as possible the joy and power of Easter in a more profound and intimate way.

The Week That Changed the World is not a mere retelling of Jesus Christ's passion and resurrection; it consists of the actual words of

1

scripture. Using Zondervan's acclaimed translation, *The Bible, Today's New International Version,* this book presents what could be considered the complete and unabridged Easter story—with an emphasis on the word *story.* It begins with John's prediction that "Jesus would die for the Jewish nation, and not only for that nation but also for the scattered children of God, to bring them together and make them one" and ends with its fulfillment, when the Holy Spirit descends to form a new community of both Jews and Gentiles. Most accounts of Christ's passion—whether books, films, or plays—stop short of the complete story, for it is not complete without Jesus' ascension into heaven and his subsequent sending of the Spirit on the Day of Pentecost. Here I seek to redress that by presenting the entire scope of Christ's passion.

✠

How This Book Was Written

Throughout I have used *Today's New International Version* of the Bible, the newest version of the NIV, a well-known and trusted translation that is both faithful to the original Greek and highly readable. This book is, after all, not intended to be a scholarly examination of the gospels, but a devotional, with no verse or chapter notations to interrupt the text. Every effort has been made to represent every word of the text, but without unnecessary or awkward repetition. At the same time, it should be noted that the style of the gospel writers often seems awkward and repetitive to most modern readers. Where the original text is repetitive, this sense has been retained in the synthesis.

A concern, however, may be justly raised: Is this Holy Scripture? In the strictest sense of the word, no. It is an artful re-presentation of scripture, using the actual texts as its basic material. But the Holy Spirit and the tradition of the early church have given us four separate accounts of Jesus' life, not one. A synthesis necessarily obscures the uniquely individual voice of the four authors, and their particular theological emphases. At the same time, we should remember that the Easter celebration is an observance of all four gospel accounts concerning the death and resurrection of Jesus, and all four accounts are used in worship services, books, and films concerning the events of Holy Week. With that in mind, this book is meant to provide the most accurate and holistic kind of Easter meditation, using to the fullest extent the actual words of the four evangelists.

There have been many harmonizations of the gospels in the past, going as far back as Tatian's *Diatessaron* in the second century, all with varying degrees of success. In fact, many scholars today see the gospels of Matthew and Luke as the first attempts at a harmonization, being composites of earlier written sources, including Mark, and oral traditions—Luke says this much at the beginning of his gospel. My hope is that my synthesis will inspire you to return to the four gospels with renewed interest and understanding. By becoming familiar with what all four evangelists present together, we can better see which details each gospel focuses on (and which ones are left out), depending on their main themes.

The chronological arrangement was in itself no small task. Where the correct placement of a certain event in time seemed ambiguous, I consulted contemporary biblical scholarship as well as the church's traditions: where, and on what day, has the church since ancient times placed a certain event? Only in a very few instances, where there was no clear indication, did I take artistic license. It should be kept in mind, however, that this book is not an attempt to present a definitive account of "what really happened and how," which stands behind almost all previous harmonizations. It is an attempt to represent all of the traditions of Christ's passion, whether explicit in scripture or in the order of various Easter celebrations, as one seamless narrative for the purpose of Lenten and Easter devotions.

The Gospel of Mark is given special prominence, since it is generally assumed to be the oldest, and I used it as a template for the flow of events. Whichever passage contained the most detail, however, usually won out. Since John's account of Jesus' anointing at Bethany contains far more specific detail than the other three, for example, it is used as the definitive account. The details that are unique to Matthew, Mark, and Luke were then imported into John's account.

In what appear to be incompatible accounts of a single event, every benefit of the doubt is given. Thus I assumed that two competing accounts were both valid, and retained the details unique to both. So when Matthew reports that two angels appeared at the resurrection, but Mark only has one, the synthesis has two. Furthermore, if the gospel accounts have seemingly irreconcilable statements in the text, I use both rather than favoring one over the other—seeing them as complementary rather than contradictory. One example of this is the exact time of the crucifixion. John says that Jesus was condemned before Pilate at "about noon," while Mark places the crucifixion at "nine in the morning." I have left both statements intact, assuming that the crucifixion occurred sometime between nine in the morning and noon.

✣

HOW TO USE THIS BOOK

There are many ways of reading this book. The first and most important is reading it day by day during Holy Week, following along as the events happened. Begin by reading chapter one on the Friday before Palm Sunday (mark your calendar!) to prepare yourself for the week ahead. On Saturday, read chapter two. The next day, Palm Sunday, you are now in a real-time account of Holy Week and will remain there until the end of Easter Sunday. When Holy Week is over, read the accounts of the Ascension and of Pentecost on the Monday and Tuesday following Easter to help keep the joyful memory of Easter Sunday alive throughout the weeks following Easter. This means, simply put, that you'll be spending twelve consecutive days reading through the book, from two days before Palm Sunday to two days after Easter Sunday.

Although this daily reading plan is the primary intention for this book, there are many other useful ways of reading it.

✣ The chapters may, of course, be read at any time of the year, as quickly or slowly as desired, alone or in a group.

✣ The readings may serve as a launching pad for a more in-depth study of the four individual gospels.

✣ The first two chapters may be read during Hanukkah or Christmas, the middle chapters during Lent, and the last two chapters during the Easter season and Pentecost.

✣ The readings may also be a useful Lenten devotional, either for a small group or an individual. The book may be divided into a forty-day reading plan to reflect the forty days of Lent, or a fifty-day reading plan, corresponding to the fifty days from Easter to Pentecost.

✣ Some readers may find it help to write their own short meditations, prayers, or reflection questions to accompany each chapter or section.

To complement the reading of the daily events of Holy Week, there are four additional elements that accompany each chapter: an introduction, a reading from scripture, a reading from ancient Christian tradition, and a prayer. Each chapter opens with an introduction that sets the stage and connects each day's events to the rest of the story. The scripture readings that follow the gospel account for that day have traditional associations with Holy Week and greatly enhance our observance because they place the events in the greater context of biblical teaching and prophecy as a whole. Through these readings we catch a glimpse of the profound unity of scripture, and of the mysterious workings of God's plan for his people throughout space and time. A reading from the church's tradition, entitled "Ancient Wisdom," then follows.* These writings from the early centuries of Christian history provide a powerful counterpoint to the scriptural text written by our ancestors in the faith through the centuries since the first Holy Week. Finally, each chapter ends with a prayer chosen from the liturgical resources of the Episcopal Church, including the 1979 *Book of Common Prayer, The Book of Occasional Services,* and *Lesser Feasts and Fasts.*

I invite you to join Jesus and the disciples in walking the road that leads to Jerusalem, that you may fully enter into the mystery of the death and resurrection of our Lord and Savior, and may be transformed by this journey. The idea is to observe firsthand, as it were, Jesus' battle and ultimate victory over death, evil, and suffering. May it usher you into a deeper and more powerful observance of the Easter holiday, and may it draw you closer to God and neighbor.

* The readings have been selected from two sources: *The Liturgy of the Hours: According to the Roman Rite,* Volumes I and II, English translation prepared by the International Commission on English in the Liturgy (New York: Catholic Book Publishing, Inc., 1976); and *Catechism of the Catholic Church: Second Edition,* trans. United States Catholic Conference, Inc. (Citta del Vaticano: Libreria Artitrice Vaticana, 1994, 1997).

THE WEEK THAT CHANGED THE WORLD

As high priest that year, Caiaphas prophesied that Jesus would die for the Jewish nation, and not only for that nation but also for the scattered children of God, to bring them together and make them one.

(John 11:51–52)

CHAPTER ONE

The Raising of Lazarus

Our story begins in December. Jesus is in the temple courts in Jerusalem for the Hanukkah festival, which celebrates God's deliverance of Israel from Greek oppression and the rededication of the temple after it was desecrated by the Greeks. Many of the women and men who followed Jesus are gathered here among the massive pillars of Solomon's Colonnade, bracing themselves against the cold. They watch as Jesus paces back and forth in front of the religious leaders, his voice echoing off the polished stone, and they listen.

It is here in the temple, in this moment, that Jesus barely escapes being stoned to death for his radical claim to be Israel's Messiah. It will be his last visit to the temple until the events of Holy Week. After this confrontation, he and his disciples leave Judea to take refuge in Perea, a district on the eastern side of the Jordan River, far from the tempestuous climate of Jerusalem.

The gospels do not tell us much about those dark winter months, only that a short time later, Jesus' friend Lazarus died. Even though Bethany, the home of Lazarus, lies within walking distance of Jerusalem, Jesus went there to bring back his friend.

Within these two events we find the themes of death and resurrection, of decay and rebirth—themes that will continue throughout the rest of the story.

Now the Festival of Dedication had come at Jerusalem. It was winter, and Jesus was in the temple courts walking in Solomon's Colonnade. The people there came and gathered around him, saying, "How long will you keep us in suspense? If you are the Messiah, tell us plainly."

Jesus answered, "I did tell you, but you do not believe. The works I do in my Father's name testify about me, but you do not believe because you are not my sheep. My sheep listen to my voice; I know them, and they follow me. I give them eternal life, and they shall never perish; no one will snatch them out of my hand. My Father, who has given them to me, is greater than all; no one can snatch them out of my Father's hand. I and the Father are one."

They picked up stones to stone him, but Jesus said to them, "I have shown you many good works from the Father. For which of these do you stone me?"

"We are not stoning you for any good work," they replied, "but for blasphemy, because you, a mere man, claim to be God."

Jesus answered them, "Is it not written in your Law, 'I have said you are "gods"'? If he called them 'gods,' to whom the word of God came—and Scripture cannot be broken—what about the one whom the Father set apart as his very own and sent into the world? Why then do you accuse me of blasphemy because I said 'I am God's Son'? Do not believe me unless I do the works of my Father. But if I do them, even though you do not believe me, believe the works, that you may know and understand that the Father is in me, and I in the Father." Again they tried to seize him, but he escaped their grasp.

Then Jesus went back across the Jordan to the place where John had been baptizing in the early days. Here he stayed and many people came to him. They said, "Though John never performed a sign, all that John said about this man was true." And in that place many believed in Jesus.

Now a man named Lazarus was sick. He was from Bethany, the village of Mary and her sister Martha. (This Mary, whose brother Lazarus now lay sick, was the same one who poured perfume on the

Lord and wiped his feet with her hair.) So the sisters sent word to Jesus, "Lord, the one you love is sick."

When he heard this, Jesus said, "This sickness will not end in death. No, it is for God's glory so that God's Son may be glorified through it." Now Jesus loved Martha and her sister and Lazarus. So when he heard that Lazarus was sick, he stayed where he was two more days, and then he said to his disciples, "Let us go back to Judea."

"But Rabbi," they said, "a short while ago the Jews there tried to stone you, and yet you are going back?"

Jesus answered, "Are there not twelve hours of daylight? Those who walk in the daytime will not stumble, for they see by this world's light. It is when people walk at night that they stumble, for they have no light."

After he had said this, he went on to tell them, "Our friend Lazarus has fallen asleep; but I am going there to wake him up."

His disciples replied, "Lord, if he sleeps, he will get better." Jesus had been speaking of his death, but his disciples thought he meant natural sleep.

So then he told them plainly, "Lazarus is dead, and for your sake I am glad I was not there, so that you may believe. But let us go to him."

Then Thomas (also known as Didymus) said to the rest of the disciples, "Let us also go, that we may die with him."

Now as Jesus started on his way, a certain ruler ran up to him and fell on his knees before him. "Good teacher," he asked, "what good thing must I do to inherit eternal life?"

"Why do you call me good?" Jesus answered. "And why do you ask me about what is good? No one is good—except God alone. If you want to enter life, keep the commandments."

"Which ones?" he inquired.

Jesus replied, "You know the commandments: 'You shall not murder, you shall not commit adultery, you shall not steal, you shall not give false testimony, you shall not defraud, honor your father and mother,' and 'love your neighbor as yourself.'"

"Teacher," the young man declared, "all these I have kept since I was a boy. What do I still lack?"

When Jesus heard this, he looked at him and loved him.

"You still lack one thing," Jesus answered. "If you want to be perfect, go, sell everything you have and give to the poor, and you will have treasure in heaven. Then come, follow me."

When the young man heard this, his face fell. He went away very sad, because he had great wealth.

Then Jesus looked around and said to his disciples, "Truly I tell you, it is hard for the rich to enter the kingdom of heaven."

The disciples were amazed at his words. But Jesus said again, "Children, how hard it is to enter the kingdom of God! Indeed, it is easier for a camel to go through the eye of a needle than for the rich to enter the kingdom of God."

When the disciples heard this, they were even more amazed, and said to each other, "Who then can be saved?"

Jesus looked at them and said, "With human beings this is impossible, but not with God; all things are possible with God."

Peter said to him, "We have left everything to follow you! What then will there be for us?"

"Truly I tell you," Jesus replied, "at the renewal of all things, when the Son of Man sits on his glorious throne, you who have followed me will also sit on twelve thrones, judging the twelve tribes of Israel. And no one who has left home or wife or brothers or sisters or mother or father or children or fields for my sake, and for the gospel of the kingdom of God, will fail to receive a hundred times as much in this present age: homes, brothers, sisters, mothers, children and fields—along with persecutions—and in the age to come, eternal life. But many who are first will be last, and many who are last will be first."

"For the kingdom of heaven is like a landowner who went out early in the morning to hire workers for his vineyard. He agreed to pay them a denarius for the day and sent them into his vineyard.

"About nine in the morning he went out and saw others standing in the marketplace doing nothing. He told them, 'You also go and work in my vineyard, and I will pay you whatever is right.' So they went.

"He went out again about noon and about three in the afternoon and did the same thing. About five in the afternoon he went out and found still others standing around. He asked them, 'Why have you been standing here all day long doing nothing?'

"'Because no one has hired us,' they answered.

"He said to them, 'You also go and work in my vineyard.'

"When evening came, the owner of the vineyard said to his supervisor, 'Call the workers and pay them their wages, beginning with the last ones hired and going on to the first.'

"The workers who were hired about five in the afternoon came and each received a denarius. So when those came who were hired first, they expected to receive more. But each one of them also received a denarius. When they received it, they began to grumble against the landowner. 'These men who were hired last worked only one hour,' they said, 'and you have made them equal to us who have borne the burden of the work and the heat of the day.'

"But he answered one of them, 'Friend, I am not being unfair to you. Didn't you agree to work for a denarius? Take your pay and go. I want to give the one who was hired last the same as I gave you. Don't I have the right to do what I want with my own money? Or are you envious because I am generous?'

"So the last will be first, and the first will be last."

On his arrival, Jesus found that Lazarus had already been in the tomb for four days. Now Bethany was less than two miles from Jerusalem, and many Jews had come to Martha and Mary to comfort them in the loss of their brother. When Martha heard that Jesus was coming, she went out to meet him, but Mary stayed at home.

"Lord," Martha said to Jesus, "if you had been here, my brother would not have died. But I know that even now God will give you whatever you ask."

Jesus said to her, "Your brother will rise again."

Martha answered, "I know he will rise again in the resurrection at the last day."

Jesus said to her, "I am the resurrection and the life. Anyone who believes in me will live, even though they die; and whoever lives by believing in me will never die. Do you believe this?"

"Yes, Lord," she told him, "I believe that you are the Messiah, the Son of God, who was to come into the world."

After she had said this, she went back and called her sister Mary aside. "The Teacher is here," she said, "and is asking for you." When Mary heard this, she got up quickly and went to him. Now Jesus had not yet entered the village, but was still at the place where Martha had met him. When the Jews who had been with Mary in the house, comforting her, noticed how quickly she got up and went out, they followed her, supposing she was going to the tomb to mourn there.

When Mary reached the place where Jesus was and saw him, she fell at his feet and said, "Lord, if you had been here, my brother would not have died."

When Jesus saw her weeping, and the Jews who had come along with her also weeping, he was deeply moved in spirit and troubled. "Where have you laid him?" he asked.

"Come and see, Lord," they replied.

Jesus wept.

Then the Jews said, "See how he loved him!"

But some of them said, "Could not he who opened the eyes of the blind man have kept this man from dying?"

Jesus, once more deeply moved, came to the tomb. It was a cave with a stone laid across the entrance. "Take away the stone," he said.

"But, Lord," said Martha, the sister of the dead man, "by this time there is a bad odor, for he has been there four days."

Then Jesus said, "Did I not tell you that if you believe, you will see the glory of God?"

So they took away the stone. Then Jesus looked up and said, "Father, I thank you that you have heard me. I knew that you always hear me, but I said this for the benefit of the people standing here, that they may believe that you sent me."

When he had said this, Jesus called out in a loud voice, "Lazarus, come out!" The dead man came out, his hands and feet wrapped with strips of linen, and a cloth around his face.

Jesus said to them, "Take off the grave clothes and let him go."

Therefore many of the Jews who had come to visit Mary, and had seen what Jesus did, put their faith in him. But some of them went to the Pharisees and told them what Jesus had done. Then the chief priests and the Pharisees called a meeting of the Sanhedrin.

"What are we accomplishing?" they asked. "Here is this man performing many signs. If we let him go on like this, everyone will believe in him, and then the Romans will come and take away both our temple and our nation."

Then one of them, named Caiaphas, who was high priest that year, spoke up, "You know nothing at all! You do not realize that it is better for you that one man die for the people than that the whole nation perish."

He did not say this on his own, but as high priest that year he prophesied that Jesus would die for the Jewish nation, and not only for that nation but also for the scattered children of God, to bring them together and make them one. So from that day on they plotted to take his life.

Therefore Jesus no longer moved about publicly among the Jews. Instead he withdrew to a region near the wilderness, to a village called Ephraim, where he stayed with his disciples.

In today's lectionary reading from the Psalms, David sings a song of praise to God for delivering him from Saul, who sought to kill him. Here we find a trust in God that parallels Jesus' trust in his heavenly Father. Though the Father will not always protect Jesus from death, just as many holy servants who lived before Jesus were killed, this psalm expresses a trust in God's love that is unshakable. This psalm also offers a subtle indication of David's hope in a future resurrection. We could well imagine this prayer coming from the mouth of the risen Lazarus.

✠ PSALM 18:1–6

I love you, LORD, my strength.

The LORD is my rock, my fortress and my deliverer;
my God is my rock, in whom I take refuge,
my shield and the horn of my salvation, my stronghold.

I called to the LORD, who is worthy of praise,
and I have been saved from my enemies.

The cords of death entangled me;
the torrents of destruction overwhelmed me.

The cords of the grave coiled around me;
the snares of death confronted me.

In my distress I called to the LORD;
I cried to my God for help.

From his temple he heard my voice;
my cry came before him, into his ears.

Ancient Wisdom from Fulgentius of Ruspe

The sacrifices of animal victims which our forefathers were commanded to offer to God by the holy Trinity itself, the one God of the old and new testaments, foreshadowed the most acceptable gift of all. This was the offering which in his compassion the only Son of God would make of himself in his human nature for our sake....

He is the priest through whom we have been reconciled, the sacrifice by which we have been reconciled, the temple in which we have been reconciled, the God with whom we have been reconciled. He alone is priest, sacrifice and temple because he is all these things as God in the form of a servant; but he is not alone as God, for he is this with the Father and the Holy Spirit in the form of God.

Almighty and most merciful God, drive from us all weakness of body, mind, and spirit; that, being restored to wholeness, we may with free hearts become what you intend us to be and accomplish what you want us to do; through Jesus Christ our Lord, who lives and reigns with you and the Holy Spirit, one God, for ever and ever. Amen.

✠

CHAPTER TWO

The Road to Jerusalem

The first month of the religious calendar, Nisan, was the most important month for Jews. It was the month of the Passover festival, the greatest festival of the year. The book of Exodus commanded that the Passover be observed on the fourteenth day of Nisan, at the beginning of springtime. Passover was the focal point of the Jewish year, and it is the focal point of the Easter story. Passover Day would immediately be followed by seven days of eating unleavened bread, from the fifteenth to the twenty-first of Nisan. The festival of Unleavened Bread officially marked the beginning of the barley harvest, and it commemorated Israel's exile from Egypt.

Although Passover is two weeks away, falling this year on a Friday, observant Jews want to get to Jerusalem a week early for the ceremony of cleansing by which they will be made ritually pure in order to eat the sacred Passover meal. They have to be in Jerusalem to receive the holy water that contains the ashes of a red heifer sacrificed by the temple priests. This second week of Nisan is to be a time of thoughtful reflection, somewhat as Lent is for us today.

From the very first day of Nisan, there are several hundred thousand pilgrims on the march to the houses, hotels, and camps in and around Jerusalem. It is at this time that Jesus and his disciples leave the small village of Ephraim and, on their final journey together, take one of the many dusty paths that wind their way through the Judean hills.

Amid the dizzying rush of the crowds, the noise of bleating goats and sheep, and the raucous play of children, the disciples' hearts race with nervous energy. They sense something amazing is about to happen, but they aren't sure exactly what.

Their rabbi and hoped-for messiah seems to be unusually moody and unpredictable. He is talking about death and betrayal, about losing everything. And he is speaking of a kingdom that cannot possibly function, let alone stand up to the oppressive might of the Roman Empire.

The disciples are anxiously aware that everyone who has heard and seen Jesus, and those from distant lands who have only heard of him, will be looking for him. Ready or not, they are about to take center stage.

When it was almost time for the Jewish Passover, many went up from the country to Jerusalem for their ceremonial cleansing before the Passover. They kept looking for Jesus, and as they stood in the temple courts they asked one another, "What do you think? Isn't he coming to the Festival at all?" But the chief priests and Pharisees had given orders that anyone who found out where Jesus was should report it so that they might arrest him.

Now Jesus was going up to Jerusalem, leading the way, and the disciples were astonished, while those who followed were afraid. Again he took the twelve disciples aside and told them what was going to happen to him. "We are going up to Jerusalem," he said, "and everything that is written by the prophets about the Son of Man will be fulfilled. He will be delivered over to the chief priests and the teachers of the law. They will condemn him to death and will hand him over to the Gentiles, who will mock him, insult him, spit on him, flog him and crucify him. On the third day he will be raised to life."

The disciples did not understand any of this. Its meaning was hidden from them, and they did not know what he was talking about.

Then the mother of Zebedee's sons came to Jesus with her sons, James and John, and, kneeling down, asked a favor of him.

"Teacher," she said, "we want you to do for us whatever we ask."

"What do you want me to do for you?" he asked.

She replied, "Grant that one of these two sons of mine may sit at your right and the other at your left in your kingdom."

"You don't know what you are asking," Jesus said to them. "Can you drink the cup I am going to drink or be baptized with the baptism I am baptized with?"

"We can," they answered.

Jesus said to them, "You will indeed drink from the cup I drink and be baptized with the baptism I am baptized with, but to sit at my right or left is not for me to grant. These places belong to those for whom they have been prepared by my Father."

When the ten heard about this, they became indignant with the two brothers, James and John. Jesus called them together and said, "You know that those who are regarded as rulers of the Gentiles lord it over them, and their high officials exercise authority over them. Not so with you. Instead, whoever wants to become great among you must be your servant, and whoever wants to be first must be slave of all. For even the Son of Man did not come to be served, but to serve, and to give his life as a ransom for many."

Then they came to Jericho. As Jesus and his disciples approached Jericho, a large crowd followed him. Two blind men were sitting by the roadside begging. When one of them, Bartimaeus (that is, the Son of Timaeus), heard the crowd going by, he asked what was happening. They told him, "Jesus of Nazareth is passing by."

When he heard that it was Jesus of Nazareth, he began to shout, "Lord Jesus, Son of David, have mercy on us!" The crowd who led the way rebuked him and told him to be quiet, but he shouted all the louder, "Lord, Son of David, have mercy on us!"

Jesus stopped and ordered the man to be brought to him, saying, "Call him." So they called to the blind man, "Cheer up! On your feet! He's calling you." Throwing his cloak aside, he jumped to his feet and came to Jesus. When he came near, Jesus asked him, "What do you want me to do for you?"

The blind man answered, "Rabbi, we want to see." Jesus had compassion on them and touched their eyes. "Receive your sight," Jesus said to them. "Go, your faith has healed you." Immediately they received their sight and followed Jesus along the road, praising God. When all the people saw it, they also praised God.

Jesus entered Jericho and was passing through. A man was there by the name of Zacchaeus; he was a chief tax collector and was wealthy. He wanted to see who Jesus was, but because he was short

19

he could not see over the crowd. So he ran ahead and climbed a sycamore-fig tree to see him, since Jesus was coming that way.

When Jesus reached the spot, he looked up and said to him, "Zacchaeus, come down immediately. I must stay at your house today." So he came down at once and welcomed him gladly.

All the people saw this and began to mutter, "He has gone to be the guest of a 'sinner.'"

But Zacchaeus stood up and said to the Lord, "Look, Lord! Here and now I give half of my possessions to the poor, and if I have cheated anybody out of anything, I will pay back four times the amount."

Jesus said to him, "Today salvation has come to this house, because this man, too, is a son of Abraham. For the Son of Man came to seek and to save what was lost."

While they were listening to this, he went on to tell them a parable, because he was near Jerusalem and the people thought that the kingdom of God was going to appear at once. He said: "A man of noble birth went to a distant country to have himself appointed king and then to return. So he called ten of his servants and gave them ten minas. 'Put this money to work,' he said, 'until I come back.'

"But his subjects hated him and sent a delegation after him to say, 'We don't want this man to be our king.'

"He was made king, however, and returned home. Then he sent for the servants to whom he had given the money, in order to find out what they had gained with it.

"The first one came and said, 'Sir, your mina has earned ten more.'

"'Well done, my good servant!' his master replied. 'Because you have been trustworthy in a very small matter, take charge of ten cities.'

"The second came and said, 'Sir, your mina has earned five more.'

"His master answered, 'You take charge of five cities.'

"Then another servant came and said, 'Sir, here is your mina; I have kept it laid away in a piece of cloth. I was afraid of you, because you are a hard man. You take out what you did not put in and reap what you did not sow.'

"His master replied, 'I will judge you by your own words, you wicked servant! You knew, did you, that I am a hard man, taking out what I did not put in, and reaping what I did not sow? Why then didn't you put my money on deposit, so that when I came back, I could have collected it with interest?'

"Then he said to those standing by, 'Take his mina away from him and give it to the one who has ten minas.'

"'Sir,' they said, 'he already has ten!'

"He replied, 'I tell you that to everyone who has, more will be given, but as for those who have nothing, even what they have will be taken away. But those enemies of mine who did not want me to be king over them—bring them here and kill them in front of me.'"

After Jesus had said this, he went on ahead, going up to Jerusalem. Six days before the Passover, Jesus came to Bethany, where Lazarus lived. Meanwhile a large crowd of Jews found out that Jesus was there and came, not only because of him but also to see Lazarus, whom he had raised from the dead. So the chief priests made plans to kill Lazarus as well, for on account of him many of the Jews were going over to Jesus and putting their faith in him.

This prophecy by Ezekiel is from a time in Israel's history when all seemed lost. The conquered and exiled Israelites were held captive in Babylon, far from their homeland; and their holy city, Jerusalem, lay in ruins. These verses are songs of hope in the face of grief and uncertainty. Perhaps the prophet's promises were in the minds of the disciples as they walked the road that led to the top of the Mount of Olives, from where they could see the breathtaking glory of Jerusalem below.

In a mysterious way, the realization of these prophetic words is both "now" and "not yet." They would be fulfilled that week, just not in the way the disciples anticipated. And today we still hope for the complete fulfillment of these promises, on that day when the heavenly reality and the earthly reality will become one.

✠ EZEKIEL 37:21–28

This is what the Sovereign LORD says: I will take the Israelites out of the nations where they have gone. I will gather them from all around and bring them back into their own land. I will make them one nation in the land, on the mountains of Israel. There will be one king over all of them and they will never again be two nations or be divided into two kingdoms. They will no longer defile themselves with their idols and vile images or with any of their offenses, for I will save them from all their sinful backsliding, and I will cleanse them. They will be my people, and I will be their God.

My servant David will be king over them, and they will all have one shepherd. They will follow my laws and be careful to keep my decrees. They will live in the land I gave to my servant Jacob, the land where your ancestors lived. They and their children and their children's children will live there forever, and David my servant will be their prince forever. I will make a covenant of peace with them; it will be an everlasting covenant. I will establish them and increase their numbers, and I will put my sanctuary among them forever. My dwelling place will be with them; I will be their God, and they will be my people. Then the nations will know that I the LORD make Israel holy, when my sanctuary is among them forever.

✠ ANCIENT WISDOM FROM GREGORY NAZIANZEN

We are soon going to share in the Passover, and although we still do so only in a symbolic way, the symbolism already has more clarity than it possessed in former times because, under the law, the Passover was, if I may dare to say so, only a symbol of a symbol. Before long, however, when the Word drinks the new wine with us in the kingdom of his Father, we shall be keeping the Passover in a yet more perfect way, and with deeper understanding. He will then reveal to us and make clear what he has so far only partially disclosed. For this wine, so familiar to us now, is eternally new....

So let us take our part in the Passover prescribed by the law, not in a literal way, but according to the teaching of the Gospel.... We must now pass through the first veil and approach the second, turning our eyes toward the Holy of Holies. I will say more: we must sacrifice ourselves to God, each day and in everything we do, accepting all that happens to us for the sake of the Word, imitating his passion by our sufferings, and honoring his blood by shedding our own. We must be ready to be crucified.

O God, by your Word you marvelously carry out the work of reconciliation: Grant that in our Lenten fast we may be devoted to you with all our hearts, and united with one another in prayer and holy love; through Jesus Christ our Lord, who lives and reigns with you and the Holy Spirit, one God, for ever and ever. Amen.

CHAPTER THREE

Palm Sunday

It is Sunday morning, the ninth day of Nisan. Jesus and his disciples, along with thousands of other pilgrims and festival-goers, ascend to the top of the Mount of Olives, where they catch their first glimpse of Jerusalem. It is an awe-inspiring sight. Herod's temple, one of the largest manmade structures in the world, lies just before them. The temple mount, with its enormous platform, is almost a city unto itself. These temple courts, especially the vast open court of the Gentiles where Jesus would often teach, could hold many thousands of pilgrims. From the top of the Mount of Olives, Jesus will ride into Jerusalem on the back of a donkey. It will take him down past the Garden of Gethsemane, across the Kidron Valley, then up the slope of Mount Zion to the Golden Gate, the eastern entrance of the temple mount, where many expected the Messiah of Israel would enter.

It is a beautiful day. The subtle fragrance of desert flowers infuses the cool, arid breeze on this bright morning. By the time Jesus begins his royal procession to the eastern gate, great crowds realize something momentous is happening. They bring their cloaks and they cut palm branches to pave his way—society and nature falling before the new king.

But for anyone expecting a typical royal procession, this would have seemed a strange sight. Riding on the back of a donkey seemed more like the entrance of a lowly shepherd than a mighty king destined to return Israel to the glory days of Solomon's empire. And despite all the excitement, Jerusalem's reception of Jesus is certainly not one of unanimous welcome. The festival crowd's reaction is tumultuous, expressing everything from joyful adoration to curiosity, doubt to outright hostility. But for many of his followers, it seems the tide is turning. These were miracle days, when anything seemed possible.

Jesus and his followers aren't the only ones arriving in Jerusalem that day. On the other side of the city, Pilate, the Roman prefect of Judea, is arriving from the west with a thunderous procession of horses, soldiers, and weapons. They are there to oversee the great festival and to discourage any form of political uprising. And they have the power to punish and kill anyone who disrupts the peace.

☦

MORNING

The next day, as they approached Jerusalem and came to Bethphage and Bethany at the hill called the Mount of Olives, Jesus sent two of his disciples, saying to them, "Go to the village ahead of you, and just as you enter it, you will find a donkey tied there, with her colt by her, which no one has ever ridden. Untie them and bring them to me. If anyone asks you, 'Why are you doing this?' say, 'The Lord needs them and will send them back here shortly,' and he will send them right away."

The disciples who were sent ahead went and did just as Jesus had instructed them. They found a colt outside in the street, tied at a doorway. As they were untying it, its owners were standing there asking, "What are you doing, untying that colt?" They answered as Jesus had told them to. "The Lord needs it," they replied, and the owners let them go.

☦

MIDDAY

When they brought the donkey and the colt to Jesus, they threw their cloaks over the colt, and Jesus sat on it.

The great crowd that had come for the Festival heard that Jesus was on his way to Jerusalem. As he went along, many people spread their cloaks on the road, while others spread palm branches they had cut in the fields.

When he came near the place where the road goes down the Mount of Olives, the whole crowd of disciples began joyfully to praise God in loud voices for all the miracles they had seen. The crowds that went ahead of him and those that followed took palm branches and went out to meet him, shouting,

"Hosanna!"

"Hosanna to the Son of David!"

"Blessed is he who comes in the name of the Lord!"

"Blessed is the coming kingdom of our father David!"

"Blessed is the king of Israel!"

"Hosanna in the highest heaven!"

"Peace in heaven and glory in the highest!"

Some of the Pharisees in the crowd said to Jesus, "Teacher, rebuke your disciples!"

"I tell you," he replied, "if they keep quiet, the stones will cry out."

This took place to fulfill what was spoken through the prophet. As it is written:

"Say to the Daughter of Zion,
  'Do not be afraid;
      see, your king comes to you,
    gentle and riding on a donkey,
      on a colt, the foal of a donkey.'"

At first his disciples did not understand all this. Only after Jesus was glorified did they realize that these things had been written about him and that these things had been done to him.

As he approached Jerusalem and saw the city, he wept over it and said, "If you, even you, had only known on this day what would bring you peace—but now it is hidden from your eyes. The days will come upon you when your enemies will build an embankment against you and encircle you and hem you in on every side. They will dash you to the ground, you and the children within your walls. They will not leave one stone on another, because you did not recognize the time of God's coming to you."

When Jesus entered Jerusalem and went to the temple courts, he looked around at everything. The whole city was stirred and asked, "Who is this?"

The crowds answered, "This is Jesus, the prophet from Nazareth in Galilee."

✠

AFTERNOON

Now the crowd that was with him when he called Lazarus from the tomb and raised him from the dead continued to spread the word. Many people, because they had heard that he had performed this sign, went out to meet him. So the Pharisees said to one another, "See, this is getting us nowhere. Look how the whole world has gone after him!"

Now there were some Greeks among those who went up to worship at the Festival. They came to Philip, who was from Bethsaida in Galilee, with a request. "Sir," they said, "we would like to see Jesus." Philip went to tell Andrew; Andrew and Philip in turn told Jesus.

Jesus replied, "The hour has come for the Son of Man to be glorified. Very truly I tell you, unless a kernel of wheat falls to the ground and dies, it remains only a single seed. But if it dies, it produces many seeds. Those who love their life will lose it, while those who hate their life in this world will keep it for eternal life. Whoever serves me must follow me; and where I am, my servant also will be. My Father will honor the one who serves me."

"Now my soul is troubled, and what shall I say? 'Father, save me from this hour'? No, it was for this very reason I came to this hour. Father, glorify your name!"

Then a voice came from heaven, "I have glorified it, and will glorify it again." The crowd that was there and heard it said it had thundered; others said an angel had spoken to him.

Jesus said, "This voice was for your benefit, not mine. Now is the time for judgment on this world; now the prince of this world will be driven out. And I, when I am lifted up from the earth, will draw all people to myself." He said this to show the kind of death he was going to die.

The crowd spoke up, "We have heard from the Law that the Messiah will remain forever, so how can you say, 'The Son of Man must be lifted up'? Who is this 'Son of Man'?"

Then Jesus told them, "You are going to have the light just a little while longer. Walk while you have the light, before darkness overtakes you. Those who walk in the dark do not know where they are going. Put your trust in the light while you have the light,

27

so that you may become children of light." When he had finished speaking, Jesus left and hid himself from them.

Even after Jesus had performed so many signs in their presence, they still would not believe in him. This was to fulfill the word of Isaiah the prophet:

"Lord, who has believed our message
and to whom has the arm of the Lord
been revealed?"

For this reason they could not believe, because, as Isaiah says elsewhere:

"He has blinded their eyes
and hardened their hearts,
so they can neither see with their eyes,
nor understand with their hearts,
nor turn—and I would heal them."

Isaiah said this because he saw Jesus' glory and spoke about him.

Yet at the same time many even among the leaders believed in him. But because of the Pharisees they would not openly acknowledge their faith for fear they would be put out of the synagogue; for they loved human glory more than the glory of God.

Then Jesus cried out, "Those who believe in me do not believe in me only, but in the one who sent me. When they look at me, they see the one who sent me. I have come into the world as a light, so that no one who believes in me should stay in darkness.

"As for those who hear my words but do not keep them, I do not judge them. For I did not come to judge the world, but to save the world. There is a judge for those who reject me and do not accept my words; the very word I have spoken will condemn them at the last day. For I did not speak on my own, but the Father who sent me commanded me to say all that I have spoken. I know that his command leads to eternal life. So whatever I say is just what the Father has told me to say."

✟

EVENING

Since it was already late, he went out to Bethany with the Twelve. Every day Jesus was teaching at the temple, and each evening he went out to spend the night on the hill called the Mount of Olives, and all the people came early in the morning to hear him at the temple. But the chief priests, the teachers of the law and the leaders among the people were trying to kill him. Yet they could not find any way to do it, because all the people hung on his words.

✠

"Messiah"—or "Christ" in Greek—is a Hebrew word meaning "anointed." Jesus' claim to be the Messiah of Israel would result in his death. Jesus the Christ would receive his kingdom not through power, but through suffering and complete surrender to his Father's plan. It is his willingness to take up the cross on our behalf that definitively revealed Jesus as the Anointed One—our Prophet, Priest, and King. This psalm is traditionally read as part of the ancient Liturgy of the Palms as Jesus enters Jerusalem and prepares for his passion.

✠ PSALM 118:1–2, 19–29

Give thanks to the LORD, for he is good;
  his love endures forever.

Let Israel say:
  "His love endures forever."

Open for me the gates of the righteous;
  I will enter and give thanks to the LORD.

This is the gate of the LORD
  through which the righteous may enter.

I will give you thanks, for you answered me;
  you have become my salvation.

The stone the builders rejected
  has become the cornerstone;

the LORD has done this,
  and it is marvelous in our eyes.

The LORD has done it this very day;
  let us rejoice today and be glad.

LORD, save us!
  LORD, grant us success!

Blessed is he who comes in the name of the LORD.
From the house of the LORD we bless you.

The LORD is God,
and he has made his light shine on us.

With boughs in hand, join in the festal procession
up to the horns of the altar.

You are my God, and I will praise you;
you are my God, and I will exalt you.

Give thanks to the LORD, for he is good;
his love endures forever.

✠ ANCIENT WISDOM FROM ANDREW OF CRETE

Let us go together to meet Christ on the Mount of Olives. Today he returns from Bethany and proceeds of his own free will toward his holy and blessed passion, to consummate the mystery of our salvation. He who came down from heaven to raise us from the depths of sin, to raise us with himself, we are told in Scripture, *above every sovereignty, authority and power, and every other name that can be named,* now comes of his own free will to make his journey to Jerusalem. He comes without pomp or ostentation. As the psalmist says: *He will not dispute or raise his voice to make it heard in the streets.* He will be meek and humble, and he will make his entry in simplicity.

Let us run to accompany him as he hastens toward his passion, and imitate those who met him then, not by covering his path with garments, olive branches or palms, but by doing all we can to prostrate ourselves before him by being humble and by trying to live as he would wish. Then we shall be able to receive the Word at his coming, and God, whom no limits can contain, will be within us.

O Lord, strong and mighty, Lord of hosts and King of glory: Cleanse our hearts from sin, keep our hands pure, and turn our minds from what is passing away; so that at the last we may stand in your holy place and receive your blessing; through Jesus Christ our Lord, who lives and reigns with you and the Holy Spirit, one God, for ever and ever. Amen.

CHAPTER FOUR

Monday

It is the tenth day of Nisan, the day on which, long ago, Moses com-
manded the captive Israelites to procure a sacrificial lamb for each
family. They were to keep it until the fourteenth day, when it would
be slaughtered at sunset. During the intervening days the Israelites
were to pack up and get ready for their flight from Egypt. Today is
also one of the two days during the week of purification when festival-
goers are to be cleansed with the holy water. The final water cleans-
ing will occur Friday morning, just before the Passover lambs are to
be slaughtered.

Jesus will perform his own kind of cleansing today. Many pilgrims
have brought their Passover animals with them, while others will go
into the city on this day of procurement to purchase them, one animal
for every ten people. In the spacious temple courts there are those
quick to capitalize on this need—some selling doves and sheep, oth-
ers exchanging foreign currency for the pilgrims, and keeping a gen-
erous percentage.

This infuriates Jesus. What happens next is a chaotic scene: doves
escaping to their freedom, coins flying everywhere as people scramble
to pick them up—a scene that does not impress the temple authorities
or the Roman officers assigned to keep the peace.

If the disciples thought Jesus had behaved strangely before, it is
nothing compared to today's events. Their prophet seems to be losing
his mind. In the past he had tried to hide the fact that he was in
Jerusalem and often urged the people he healed not to tell anyone.
Now he is healing out in the open, in full view of the crowds.

To the disciples, this recklessness is at once thrilling and unsettling. And yet, many are seeing for the first time; many are walking a path that hadn't existed until now.

DAWN

Early the next morning, as he was leaving Bethany on his way back to the city, Jesus was hungry. Seeing in the distance a fig tree in leaf by the road, he went up to find out if it had any fruit. When he reached it, he found nothing on it except leaves, because it was not the season for figs. Then he said to the tree, "May no one ever eat fruit from you again!" And his disciples heard him say it. Immediately the tree withered.

MORNING

On reaching Jerusalem, Jesus entered the temple courts and began driving out all those who were buying and selling there. He overturned the tables of the money changers and the benches of those selling doves, and would not allow anyone to carry merchandise through the temple courts. And as he taught them, he said, "Is it not written: 'My house will be called a house of prayer for all nations'? But you have made it 'a den of robbers.'"

The chief priests and the teachers of the law heard this and began looking for a way to kill him, for they feared him, because the whole crowd was amazed at his teaching.

MIDDAY

The blind and the lame came to him at the temple, and he healed them. But when the chief priests and the teachers of the law saw the wonderful things he did and the children shouting in the temple courts, "Hosanna to the Son of David," they were indignant.

"Do you hear what these children are saying?" they asked him.

"Yes," replied Jesus, "have you never read,

"'From the lips of children and infants
    you have ordained praise'?"

EVENING

And when evening came, Jesus and his disciples went out of the city to Bethany, where they spent the night.

As we read this passage from the Letter to the Hebrews we can imagine Jesus in the temple as the definitive Passover sacrifice, standing among the sacrificial animals as he confronts and expels the money-changers.

✝ HEBREWS 9:11–15

When Christ came as high priest of the good things that are now already here, he went through the greater and more perfect tabernacle that is not made with human hands, that is to say, is not a part of this creation. He did not enter by means of the blood of goats and calves; but he entered the Most Holy Place once for all by his own blood, thus obtaining eternal redemption. The blood of goats and bulls and the ashes of a heifer sprinkled on those who are ceremonially unclean sanctify them so that they are outwardly clean. How much more, then, will the blood of Christ, who through the eternal Spirit offered himself unblemished to God, cleanse our consciences from acts that lead to death, so that we may serve the living God! For this reason Christ is the mediator of a new covenant, that those who are called may receive the promised eternal inheritance—now that he has died as a ransom to set them free from the sins committed under the first covenant.

ANCIENT WISDOM FROM CYRIL OF JERUSALEM

We do not preach only one coming of Christ, but a second as well, much more glorious than the first. The first coming was marked by patience; the second will bring the crown of a divine kingdom.

In general, what relates to our Lord Jesus Christ has two aspects. There is a birth from God before the ages, and a birth from a virgin at the fullness of time. There is a hidden coming, like that of rain on fleece, and a coming before all eyes, still in the future.

At the first coming he was wrapped in swaddling clothes in a manger. At his second coming he will be clothed in light as in a garment. In the first coming he endured the cross, despising the shame; in the second coming he will be in glory, escorted by an army of angels. We look then beyond the first coming and await the second. At the first coming we said: *Blessed is he who comes in the name of the Lord.* At the second we shall say it again; we shall go out with the angels to meet the Lord and cry out in adoration: *Blessed is he who comes in the name of the Lord.*

O God, you so loved the world that you gave your only-begotten Son to reconcile earth with heaven: Grant that we, loving you above all things, may love our friends in you, and our enemies for your sake; through Jesus Christ our Lord, who lives and reigns with you and the Holy Spirit, one God, for ever and ever. Amen.

✠

CHAPTER FIVE

Tuesday

Today Jesus goes to the temple mount again to teach the crowds for the last time. Whereas yesterday's scene was pandemonium, today the temple courts are dead silent as many thousands listen and watch as the religious authorities challenge this notorious young rabbi who teaches in parables. His arguments with the religious leaders and experts of scripture delight some and infuriate others. Yesterday he was overturning the marketplace; today he seems to be overturning their entire world.

Jesus' fierce diatribe against the religious leaders, supremely confident they are on God's side, may have seemed startling to the disciples and to the crowds. But it is not a vindictive ferocity, rather the anger of a lioness protecting her cubs.

As evening approaches, Jesus leads the disciples to the Mount of Olives, where he speaks in words that are even more severe. While they watch the limestone walls of Jerusalem turn blood-red under the setting sun, Jesus reveals to them how the world will come to an end. For the disciples it seems like the world is already ending. His kingdom will not arrive in the way they have expected. They are no longer welcome in Jerusalem. They are outcasts now.

The Jewish days always begin at sunset. On this Tuesday evening, the twelfth day of Nisan begins, when the gospels tell us the Passover is just two days away. This night, some of the religious leaders make plans to arrest Jesus. It will have to be done before Saturday, the fifteenth day of Nisan, which is not only a Sabbath but the first solemn day of the seven-day festival of Unleavened Bread. They fear a riot will break out if he is arrested on the holiest Sabbath day of the year.

✙

EARLY MORNING

In the morning, as they went along, they saw the fig tree withered from the roots. Peter remembered and said to Jesus, "Rabbi, look! The fig tree you cursed has withered!" When the disciples saw this, they were amazed. "How did the fig tree wither so quickly?" they asked.

"Have faith in God," Jesus answered. "Truly I tell you, if you have faith and do not doubt in your heart but believe that what you say will happen, not only can you do what was done to the fig tree, but also you can say to this mountain, 'Go, throw yourself into the sea,' and it will be done for you. Therefore I tell you, whatever you ask for in prayer, believe that you have received it, and it will be yours. And when you stand praying, if you hold anything against anyone, forgive them, so that your Father in heaven may forgive you your sins."

✙

MORNING

They arrived again in Jerusalem, and Jesus entered the temple courts. While he was walking in the temple courts, teaching the people and proclaiming the good news, the chief priests, the teachers of the law and the elders of the people came up to him. "Tell us, by what authority are you doing these things?" they asked. "And who gave you authority to do this?"

Jesus replied, "I will also ask you one question. If you answer me, I will tell you by what authority I am doing these things. John's baptism—where did it come from? Was it from heaven, or of human origin? Tell me!"

They discussed it among themselves and said, "If we say, 'From heaven,' he will ask, 'Then why didn't you believe him?' But if we say, 'Of human origin'...." (They were afraid all the people would stone them, for everyone held that John really was a prophet.)

So they answered Jesus, "We don't know where it was from."

Then Jesus said, "Neither will I tell you by what authority I am doing these things."

He then began to speak to them in parables: "What do you think? There was a man who had two sons. He went to the first and said, 'Son, go and work today in the vineyard.'

"'I will not,' he answered, but later he changed his mind and went.

"Then the father went to the other son and said the same thing. He answered, 'I will, sir,' but he did not go.

"Which of the two did what his father wanted?"

"The first," they answered.

Jesus said to them, "Truly I tell you, the tax collectors and the prostitutes are entering the kingdom of God ahead of you. For John came to you to show you the way of righteousness, and you did not believe him, but the tax collectors and the prostitutes did. And even after you saw this, you did not repent and believe him."

He went on to tell the people, "Listen to another parable: There was a landowner who planted a vineyard. He put a wall around it, dug a pit in it for the winepress and built a watchtower. Then he rented the vineyard to some farmers and went away for a long time, having moved to another place. When the harvest time approached, he sent a servant to the tenants to collect from them some of the fruit of the vineyard. But the tenants seized him, beat him and sent him away empty-handed.

"Then he sent another servant to them. They struck this man on the head and treated him shamefully and sent him away empty-handed. He sent still a third, and that one they wounded, threw out and stoned. Then he sent many other servants to them, more than the first time, and the tenants treated them the same way. Some of them they beat, others they killed.

"Then the owner of the vineyard said, 'What shall I do?' He had one left to send, a son, whom he loved. He sent him last of all, saying, 'I will send my son, whom I love; perhaps they will respect him.'

"But when the tenants saw the son, they talked the matter over. 'This is the heir,' they said to one another. 'Come, let's kill him, and the inheritance will be ours.' So they took him and killed him, and threw him out of the vineyard.

"Therefore, when the owner of the vineyard comes, what will he do to those tenants?"

"He will bring those wretches to a wretched end," they replied, "and he will rent the vineyard to other tenants, who will give him his share of the crop at harvest time."

When the people heard this, they said, "May this never be!"

Jesus looked directly at them and asked, "Then what is the meaning of that which is written? Have you never read in the Scriptures:

"'The stone the builders rejected
has become the cornerstone;
the Lord has done this,
and it is marvelous in our eyes'?

"Therefore I tell you that the kingdom of God will be taken away from you and given to a people that will produce its fruit. Everyone who falls on that stone will be broken to pieces, but anyone on whom it falls will be crushed."

When the chief priests and the Pharisees, the teachers of the law and the elders, heard Jesus' parables, they looked for a way to arrest him immediately, because they knew he had spoken this parable against them. But they were afraid of the crowd because the people held that he was a prophet. So they left him and went away.

✠

MIDDAY

Jesus spoke to them again in parables, saying: "The kingdom of heaven is like a king who prepared a wedding banquet for his son. He sent his servants to those who had been invited to the banquet to tell them to come, but they refused to come.

"Then he sent some more servants and said, 'Tell those who have been invited that I have prepared my dinner: My oxen and fattened cattle have been butchered, and everything is ready. Come to the wedding banquet.'

"But they paid no attention and went off—one to his field, another to his business. The rest seized his servants, mistreated them and killed them. The king was enraged. He sent his army and destroyed those murderers and burned their city.

"Then he said to his servants, 'The wedding banquet is ready, but those I invited did not deserve to come. Go to the street corners and invite to the banquet anyone you find.' So the servants went out into the streets and gathered all the people they could find, the bad as well as the good, and the wedding hall was filled with guests.

"But when the king came in to see the guests, he noticed a man there who was not wearing wedding clothes. 'Friend,' he asked, 'how did you get in here without wedding clothes?' The man was speechless.

"Then the king told the attendants, 'Tie him hand and foot, and throw him outside, into the darkness, where there will be weeping and gnashing of teeth.'

"For many are invited, but few are chosen."

Then the Pharisees went out and laid plans to trap him in his words. Keeping a close watch on him, they sent some of their disciples to Jesus along with the Herodians—spies, who pretended to be sincere. They hoped to catch Jesus in something he said so that they might hand him over to the power and authority of the governor. So the spies came to him and questioned him: "Teacher," they said, "we know that you are a man of integrity, that you speak and teach what is right. You aren't swayed by others, because you pay no attention to who they are; but you teach the way of God in accordance with the truth. Tell us then, what is your opinion? Is it right to pay the imperial tax to Caesar or not? Should we pay or shouldn't we?"

But Jesus, knowing their evil intent, saw through their duplicity and asked them, "You hypocrites, why are you trying to trap me? Show me the coin used for paying the tax." They brought him a denarius, and he asked them, "Whose portrait is this? And whose inscription is on it?"

"Caesar's," they replied.

Then Jesus said to them, "Give back to Caesar what is Caesar's, and to God what is God's."

They were unable to trap him in what he had said there in public. And astonished by his answer, they became silent. So they left him and went away.

That same day some of the Sadducees, who say there is no resurrection, came to Jesus with a question. "Teacher," they said, "Moses wrote for us that if a man's brother dies and leaves a wife but no children, the man must marry the widow and raise up offspring for his brother. Now there were seven brothers among us. The first one married a woman and died, and since he had no children, he left his wife to his brother. The second one married the widow, but he also died, leaving no child. The same thing happened to the third brother, right on down to the seventh, who died in the same way. In fact, none of the seven left any children. Last of all, the woman died too. Now then, at the resurrection, whose wife will she be of the seven, since all of them were married to her?"

Jesus replied, "Are you not in error because you do not know the Scriptures or the power of God? The people of this age marry and are given in marriage. But those who are considered worthy of taking part in the age to come and in the resurrection from the dead will neither marry nor be given in marriage. And they can no longer die; for they will be like the angels in heaven. They are God's children, since they are children of the resurrection. Now about the resurrection of the dead—even Moses showed that the dead rise. Have you not read in the book of Moses, in the account of the burning bush, how the Lord God said to him, 'I am the God of Abraham, the God of Isaac, and the God of Jacob'? He is not the God of the dead, but of the living, for to him all are alive. You are badly mistaken!"

When the crowds heard this, they were astonished at his teaching. Some of the teachers of the law responded, "Well said, teacher!"

Hearing that Jesus had silenced the Sadducees, the Pharisees got together. One of them, an expert in the law, came and heard them debating. Noticing that Jesus had given them a good answer, he tested him with this question: "Teacher, of all the commandments in the Law, which is the greatest?"

"The most important one," Jesus answered, "is this: 'Hear, O Israel, the Lord our God, the Lord is one. Love the Lord your God with all your heart and with all your soul and with all your mind and with all your strength.' This is the first and greatest commandment. And the second is like it: 'Love your neighbor as yourself.' There is no commandment greater than these. All the Law and the Prophets hang on these two commandments."

"Well said, teacher," the man replied. "You are right in saying that God is one and there is no other but him. To love him with all your heart, with all your understanding and with all your strength, and to love your neighbor as yourself is more important than all burnt offerings and sacrifices."

When Jesus saw that he had answered wisely, he said to him, "You are not far from the kingdom of God."

✠
AFTERNOON

While Jesus was teaching in the temple courts, he asked, "Why do the teachers of the law say that the Messiah is the son of David?" Since the Pharisees were gathered together, Jesus asked them, "What do you think about the Messiah? Whose son is he?"

"The son of David," they replied.

He said to them, "How is it then that David himself, speaking by the Holy Spirit, calls him 'Lord'? For he declares in the Book of Psalms:

"'The Lord said to my Lord:
"Sit at my right hand
until I make your enemies
a footstool for your feet."'

"If David himself calls him 'Lord,' how can he be his son?"

The large crowd listened to him with delight. No one could say a word in reply, and from that day on no one dared to ask him any more questions.

Then, while all the people were listening as he taught, Jesus said to the crowds and to his disciples, "The teachers of the law and the Pharisees sit in Moses' seat. So you must be careful to do everything they tell you. But do not do what they do, for they do not practice what they preach. They tie up heavy, cumbersome loads and put them on other people's shoulders, but they themselves are not willing to lift a finger to move them.

"Beware of the teachers of the law. Everything they do is done for people to see: They make their phylacteries wide and the tassels on their garments long; they love to have the most important seats in the synagogues and the places of honor at banquets; they like to walk around in flowing robes and love to be greeted with respect in the marketplaces and to have people call them, 'Rabbi.' They devour widows' houses and for a show make lengthy prayers. These men will be punished most severely."

"But you are not to be called 'Rabbi,' for you have only one Master and you are all brothers. And do not call anyone on earth 'father,' for you have one Father, and he is in heaven. Nor are you to be called 'teacher,' for you have one Teacher, the Messiah. The greatest among you will be your servant. For those who exalt themselves will be humbled, and those who humble themselves will be exalted."

"Woe to you, teachers of the law and Pharisees, you hypocrites! You shut the door of the kingdom of heaven in people's faces. You yourselves do not enter, nor will you let those enter who are trying to.

"Woe to you, teachers of the law and Pharisees, you hypocrites! You travel over land and sea to win a single convert, then you make that convert twice as much a child of hell as you are.

"Woe to you, blind guides! You say, 'If anyone swears by the temple, it means nothing; but whoever swears by the gold of the temple is bound by the oath.' You blind fools! Which is greater: the gold, or the temple that makes the gold sacred? You also say, 'If anyone swears by the altar, it means nothing; but whoever swears by the gift on the altar is bound by the oath.' You blind men! Which is greater: the gift, or the altar that makes the gift sacred? Therefore, anyone who swears by the altar swears by it and by everything on it. And anyone who swears by the temple swears by it and by the one who dwells in it. And anyone who swears by heaven swears by God's throne and by the one who sits on it.

"Woe to you, teachers of the law and Pharisees, you hypocrites! You give a tenth of your spices—mint, dill and cumin. But you have neglected the more important matters of the law—justice, mercy and faithfulness. You should have practiced the latter, without neglecting the former. You blind guides! You strain out a gnat but swallow a camel.

"Woe to you, teachers of the law and Pharisees, you hypocrites! You clean the outside of the cup and dish, but inside they are full of greed and self-indulgence. Blind Pharisee! First clean the inside of the cup and dish, and then the outside also will be clean.

"Woe to you, teachers of the law and Pharisees, you hypocrites! You are like whitewashed tombs, which look beautiful on the outside but on the inside are full of the bones of the dead and everything unclean. In the same way, on the outside you appear to people as righteous but on the inside you are full of hypocrisy and wickedness.

"Woe to you, teachers of the law and Pharisees, you hypocrites! You build tombs for the prophets and decorate the graves of the righteous. And you say, 'If we had lived in the days of our ancestors, we would not have taken part with them in shedding the blood of the prophets.' So you testify against yourselves that you are the descendants of those who murder the prophets. Fill up, then, the measure of the sin of your ancestors!

"You snakes! You brood of vipers! How will you escape being condemned to hell?

"Therefore I am sending you prophets and sages and teachers. Some of them you will kill and crucify; others you will flog in your synagogues and pursue from town to town. And so upon you will come all the righteous blood that has been shed on earth, from the blood of righteous Abel to the blood of Zechariah son of Berekiah, whom you murdered between the temple and the altar. Truly I tell you, all this will come upon this generation.

"Jerusalem, Jerusalem, you who kill the prophets and stone those sent to you, how often I have longed to gather your children together, as a hen gathers her chicks under her wings, and you were not willing. Look, your house is left to you desolate. For I tell you, you will not see me again until you say, 'Blessed is he who comes in the name of the Lord.'"

+++

LATE AFTERNOON

Jesus sat down opposite the place where the offerings were put and watched the crowd putting their money into the temple treasury. As he looked up, he saw many rich people throw in large amounts. But he also saw a poor widow come and put in two very small copper coins, worth only a fraction of a penny.

Calling his disciples to him, Jesus said, "Truly I tell you, this poor widow has put more into the treasury than all the others. All these people gave their gifts out of their wealth; but she, out of her poverty, put in everything—all she had to live on."

Jesus left the temple and was walking away when his disciples came up to him to call his attention to its buildings. Some were remarking about how the temple was adorned with beautiful stones and with gifts dedicated to God. One of his disciples said to him, "Look, Teacher! What massive stones! What magnificent buildings!"

"Do you see all these great buildings?" replied Jesus. "Truly I tell you, as for what you see here, the time will come when not one stone will be left on another; every one of them will be thrown down."

✤

SUNSET

As Jesus was sitting on the Mount of Olives opposite the temple, Peter, James, John and Andrew came to him privately. "Teacher, tell us," they asked, "when will these things happen? And what will be the sign that your coming and the end of the age are all about to be fulfilled?"

Jesus answered them: "Watch out that no one deceives you. For many will come in my name, claiming, 'I am he, the Messiah,' and, 'The time is near,' and they will deceive many. Do not follow them. When you hear of wars and rumors of wars and uprisings, see to it that you are not alarmed. Such things must happen first, but the end will not come right away."

Then he said to them: "Nation will rise against nation, and kingdom against kingdom. There will be great earthquakes, famines and pestilences in various places, and fearful events and great signs from heaven. All these are the beginning of birth pains."

"But before all this, you will be handed over to be persecuted and put to death. You must be on your guard. They will lay hands on you and will deliver you over to the local councils and prisons, and you will be flogged in the synagogues. And you will be brought to stand before governors and kings as witnesses to them, and all on account of my name. And so you will bear testimony to me. But whenever you are arrested and brought to trial, make up your mind not to worry beforehand about what to say or how you will defend yourselves. Just say whatever is given to you at the time, for I will give you words and wisdom that none of your adversaries will be able to resist or contradict. For it is not you speaking, but the Holy Spirit.

"You will be betrayed even by parents, brothers, sisters, relatives and friends, and they will put some of you to death. Brother will betray brother to death, and a father his child. Children will rebel against their parents and have them put to death. And you will be hated by all nations because of me. At that time many will turn away from the faith and will betray and hate each other, and many false prophets will appear and deceive many people. Because of the increase of wickedness, the love of most will grow cold. But not a hair of your head will perish. Those who stand firm to the end will win life and be saved. And this gospel of the kingdom must first be preached in the whole world as a testimony to all nations, and then the end will come."

"When you see Jerusalem being surrounded by armies, you will know that its desolation is near. So when you see 'the abomination that causes desolation,' spoken of through the prophet Daniel, standing in the holy place where it does not belong—let the reader understand—then let those who are in Judea flee to the mountains, let those in the city get out, and let those in the country not enter the city. Let no one on the housetop go down or enter the house to take anything out. Let no one in the field go back to get his cloak. For this is the time of punishment in fulfillment of all that has been written. How dreadful it will be in those days for pregnant women and nursing mothers!

"Pray that your flight will not take place in winter or on the Sabbath. For those will be days of great distress, unequaled from the beginning, when God created the world, until now—and never to be equaled again. There will be great distress in the land and wrath against this people. They will fall by the sword and will be taken as prisoners to all the nations. Jerusalem will be trampled on by the Gentiles until the times of the Gentiles are fulfilled. If the Lord had not cut short those days, no one would survive. But for the sake of the elect, whom he has chosen, those days will be shortened."

"At that time if anyone says to you, 'Look, here is the Messiah!' or, 'Look, there he is!' do not believe it. For false messiahs and false prophets will appear and perform great signs and wonders to deceive, if possible, even the elect. So be on your guard. See, I have told you everything ahead of time.

"So if anyone tells you, 'There he is, out in the desert,' do not go out; or, 'Here he is, in the inner rooms,' do not believe it. For as lightning that comes from the east is visible even in the west, so will be the coming of the Son of Man. Wherever there is a carcass, there the vultures will gather."

"But immediately after the distress of those days, there will be signs in the sun, moon and stars:

"'the sun will be darkened,
    and the moon will not give its light;
the stars will fall from the sky,
    and the heavenly bodies will be shaken.'

"On earth, nations will be in anguish and perplexity at the roaring and tossing of the sea. People will faint from terror, apprehensive of what is coming on the world. At that time the sign of the Son of Man will appear in the sky, and all the peoples of the earth will mourn. They will see the Son of Man coming in the clouds of the sky, with great power and glory. And he will send his angels with a loud trumpet call, and they will gather his elect from the four winds, from the ends of the earth to the ends of the heavens. When these things begin to take place, stand up and lift up your heads, because your redemption is drawing near."

He told them this parable: "Now learn this lesson from the fig tree. Look at the fig tree and all the trees. As soon as its twigs get tender and its leaves come out, you can see for yourselves and know that summer is near. Even so, when you see all these things happening, you know that the kingdom of God is near, right at the door.

"Truly I tell you, this generation will certainly not pass away until all these things have happened. Heaven and earth will pass away, but my words will never pass away."

"But about that day or hour no one knows, not even the angels in heaven, nor the Son, but only the Father.

"Be on guard! Be alert! You do not know when that time will come. It's like a man going away: He leaves his house and puts his servants in charge, each with an assigned task, and tells the one at the door to keep watch.

"Therefore keep watch because you do not know when the owner of the house will come back—whether in the evening, or at midnight, or when the rooster crows, or at dawn. If he comes suddenly, do not let him find you sleeping. What I say to you I say to everyone: 'Watch!'"

"Be careful, or your hearts will be weighed down with dissipation, drunkenness and the anxieties of life, and that day will close on you suddenly like a trap. For it will come upon all those who live on the face of the whole earth. Be always on the watch, and pray that you may be able to escape all that is about to happen, and that you may be able to stand before the Son of Man."

"As it was in the days of Noah, so it will be at the coming of the Son of Man. For in the days before the flood, people were eating and drinking, marrying and giving in marriage, up to the day Noah entered the ark; and they knew nothing about what would happen until the flood came and took them all away. That is how it will be at the coming of the Son of Man. Two men will be in the field; one will be taken and the other left. Two women will be grinding with a hand mill; one will be taken and the other left."

"Therefore keep watch, because you do not know on what day your Lord will come. But understand this: If the owner of the house had known at what time of night the thief was coming, he would have kept watch and would not have let his house be broken into. So you also must be ready, because the Son of Man will come at an hour when you do not expect him.

"Who then is the faithful and wise servant, whom the master has put in charge of the servants in his household to give them their food at the proper time? It will be good for that servant whose master finds him doing so when he returns. Truly I tell you, he will put him in charge of all his possessions. But suppose that servant is wicked and says to himself, 'My master is staying away a long time,' and he then begins to beat his fellow servants and to eat and drink with drunkards. The master of that servant will come on a day when he does not expect him and at an hour he is not aware of. He will cut him to pieces and assign him a place with the hypocrites, where there will be weeping and gnashing of teeth."

"At that time the kingdom of heaven will be like ten virgins who took their lamps and went out to meet the bridegroom. Five of them were foolish and five were wise. The foolish ones took their lamps but did not take any oil with them. The wise, however, took oil in jars along with their lamps. The bridegroom was a long time in coming, and they all became drowsy and fell asleep.

"At midnight the cry rang out: 'Here's the bridegroom! Come out to meet him!'

"Then all the virgins woke up and trimmed their lamps. The foolish ones said to the wise, 'Give us some of your oil; our lamps are going out.'

"'No,' they replied, 'there may not be enough for both us and you. Instead, go to those who sell oil and buy some for yourselves.'

"But while they were on their way to buy the oil, the bridegroom arrived. The virgins who were ready went in with him to the wedding banquet. And the door was shut.

"Later the others also came. 'Sir! Sir!' they said. 'Open the door for us!'

"But he replied, 'Truly I tell you, I don't know you.'

"Therefore keep watch, because you do not know the day or the hour."

"Again, it will be like a man going on a journey, who called his servants and entrusted his wealth to them. To one he gave five bags of gold, to another two bags, and to another one bag, each according to his ability. Then he went on his journey. The man who had received five bags of gold went at once and put his money to work and gained five more. So also, the one with two bags of gold gained two more. But the man who had received one bag went off, dug a hole in the ground and hid his master's money.

"After a long time the master of those servants returned and settled accounts with them. The man who had received five bags of gold brought the other five. 'Master,' he said, 'you entrusted me with five bags of gold. See, I have gained five more.'

"His master replied, 'Well done, good and faithful servant! You have been faithful with a few things; I will put you in charge of many things. Come and share your master's happiness!'

"The man with two bags of gold also came. 'Master,' he said, 'you entrusted me with two bags of gold; see, I have gained two more.'

"His master replied, 'Well done, good and faithful servant! You have been faithful with a few things; I will put you in charge of many things. Come and share your master's happiness!'

"Then the man who had received one bag of gold came. 'Master,' he said, 'I knew that you are a hard man, harvesting where you have not sown and gathering where you have not scattered seed. So I was afraid and went out and hid your gold in the ground. See, here is what belongs to you.'

"His master replied, 'You wicked, lazy servant! So you knew that I harvest where I have not sown and gather where I have not scattered seed? Well then, you should have put my money on deposit with the bankers, so that when I returned I would have received it back with interest.

"'Take the bag of gold from him and give it to the one who has ten bags. For those who have will be given more, and they will have an abundance. As for those who do not have, even what they have will be taken from them. And throw that worthless servant outside, into the darkness, where there will be weeping and gnashing of teeth.'"

"When the Son of Man comes in his glory, and all the angels with him, he will sit on his glorious throne. All the nations will be gathered before him, and he will separate the people one from another as a shepherd separates the sheep from the goats. He will put the sheep on his right and the goats on his left.

"Then the King will say to those on his right, 'Come, you who are blessed by my Father; take your inheritance, the kingdom prepared for you since the creation of the world. For I was hungry and you gave me something to eat, I was thirsty and you gave me something to drink, I was a stranger and you invited me in, I needed clothes and you clothed me, I was sick and you looked after me, I was in prison and you came to visit me.'

"Then the righteous will answer him, 'Lord, when did we see you hungry and feed you, or thirsty and give you something to drink? When did we see you a stranger and invite you in, or needing clothes and clothe you? When did we see you sick or in prison and go to visit you?'

"The King will reply, 'Truly I tell you, whatever you did for one of the least of these brothers of mine, you did for me.'

"Then he will say to those on his left, 'Depart from me, you who are cursed, into the eternal fire prepared for the devil and his angels. For I was hungry and you gave me nothing to eat, I was thirsty and you gave me nothing to drink, I was a stranger and you did not invite me in, I needed clothes and you did not clothe me, I was sick and in prison and you did not look after me.'

"They also will answer, 'Lord, when did we see you hungry or thirsty or a stranger or needing clothes or sick or in prison, and did not help you?'

"He will reply, 'Truly I tell you, whatever you did not do for one of the least of these, you did not do for me.'

"Then they will go away to eternal punishment, but the righteous to eternal life."

✝

NIGHT

When Jesus had finished saying all these things, he said to his disciples, "As you know, the Passover is two days away—and the Son of Man will be handed over to be crucified."

Now the Passover and the Festival of Unleavened Bread were approaching. Then the chief priests, the teachers of the law, and the elders of the people assembled in the palace of the high priest, whose name was Caiaphas. They were looking for some sly way to arrest Jesus and kill him, for they were afraid of the people. "But not during the Festival," they said, "or the people may riot."

There are times when God seems to fail us when it comes to his promises to bless us. Why doesn't God always rescue us or protect us from evil? What value do his promises have when we feel he has abandoned us?

Jesus is an example of perfect trust in God's faithfulness, but he had to endure the rejection of these promises first. The paradox of the cross—of glory in shame, of victory in defeat, of the king of the world as the servant of all—is the greatest of paradoxes. This passage in Paul's letter to the Corinthian church reminds us of Jesus' teaching before the religious leaders and the crowds who, like us, struggled to understand his true nature and mission.

✠ 1 CORINTHIANS 1:18–25

For the message of the cross is foolishness to those who are perishing, but to us who are being saved it is the power of God. For it is written:

> "I will destroy the wisdom of the wise;
>   the intelligence of the intelligent I will frustrate."

Where are the wise? Where is the teacher of the law? Where is the philosopher of this age? Has not God made foolish the wisdom of the world? For since in the wisdom of God the world through its wisdom did not know him, God was pleased through the foolishness of what was preached to save those who believe. Jews demand signs and Greeks look for wisdom, but we preach Christ crucified: a stumbling block to Jews and foolishness to Gentiles, but to those whom God has called, both Jews and Greeks, Christ the power of God and the wisdom of God. For the foolishness of God is wiser than human wisdom, and the weakness of God is stronger than human strength.

ANCIENT WISDOM FROM AUGUSTINE OF HIPPO

The Lord, the teacher of love, full of love, came in person *with summary judgment on the world,* as had been foretold of him, and showed that the law and the prophets are summed up in two commandments of love.

Call to mind, brethren, what these two commandments are. They ought to be very familiar to you; they should not only spring to mind when I mention them, but ought never to be absent from your hearts. Keep always in mind that we must love God and our neighbor: *Love God with your whole heart, your whole soul, and your whole mind, and your neighbor as yourself.*

These two commandments must be always in your thoughts and in your hearts, treasured, acted on, fulfilled.

Almighty God our heavenly Father, renew in us the gifts of your mercy; increase our faith, strengthen our hope, enlighten our understanding, widen our charity, and make us ready to serve you; through Jesus Christ our Lord, who lives and reigns with you and the Holy Spirit, one God, for ever and ever. Amen.

CHAPTER SIX

Wednesday

*After Jesus' confrontation with the Pharisees and his apocalyptic ser-
mon the previous day, Wednesday is a quiet day of rest for the disciples away from the noise and crowding of the city. It is the calm before
the storm. They are back in the village of Bethany, staying there for
the last time. During dinner, Mary comes to Jesus with a lavish and
costly offering, a gift worthy of a king. Her sacrifice is both an act of
devotion and a foreshadowing of the inestimable price Jesus is about
to pay for the salvation of the world.*

*This night, the beginning of the thirteenth day of Nisan, Judas be-
trays Jesus to the religious authorities and makes plans with them for
his arrest—an arrest that will take place tomorrow night, the beginning of Passover.*

EVENING

While Jesus was in Bethany, a dinner was given in his honor in the home of Simon the Leper. Martha served, while Lazarus was among those reclining at the table with him.

While Jesus was reclining, Mary came to him with an alabaster jar of very expensive perfume—about a pint of pure nard. She broke the jar and poured the perfume on his head. She also poured it on Jesus' feet and wiped his feet with her hair. And the house was filled with the fragrance of the perfume.

When the disciples saw this, they were indignant. Some of those present were saying to one another, "Why this waste?" And they rebuked her harshly.

One of his disciples, Judas Iscariot, who was later to betray him, objected, "Why wasn't this perfume sold and the money given to the poor? It was worth more than a year's wages." He did not say this because he cared about the poor but because he was a thief; as keeper of the money bag, he used to help himself to what was put into it.

Aware of this, Jesus said to them, "Leave her alone. Why are you bothering this woman? She has done a beautiful thing to me. It was intended that she should save this perfume for the day of my burial. You will always have the poor among you, and you can help them any time you want. But you will not always have me.

"She did what she could. When she poured this perfume on my body, she did it to prepare me beforehand for burial. Truly I tell you, wherever this gospel is preached throughout the world, what she has done will also be told, in memory of her."

NIGHT

Then Satan entered the one called Judas Iscariot, one of the Twelve. And Judas went to the chief priests and the officers of the temple guard and discussed with them how he might betray Jesus to them. They were delighted to hear this and agreed to give him money. And Judas asked, "What are you willing to give me if I hand him over to you?" So they counted out for him thirty silver coins. He consented, and from then on Judas watched for an opportunity to hand Jesus over to them when no crowd was present.

✟

The following passage from Isaiah is the portrait of a true servant of God—a servant who is willing to be obedient "even to the point of death." It reminds us that even through the most severe trials, God is our deliverer and he will always be with us, even through death. The way of the cross is the way to victory.

✟ ISAIAH 50:4–9A

The Sovereign LORD has given me an instructed tongue,
    to know the word that sustains the weary.

He wakens me morning by morning,
    wakens my ear to listen like one being taught.

The Sovereign LORD has opened my ears;
    I have not been rebellious,
    I have not turned away.

I offered my back to those who beat me,
    my cheeks to those who pulled out my beard;
    I did not hide my face from mocking and spitting.

Because the Sovereign LORD helps me,
    I will not be disgraced.

Therefore I have set my face like flint,
    and I know I will not be put to shame.

He who vindicates me is near.
    Who then will bring charges against me?
    Let us face each other!

Who are my accusers?
    Let them confront me!

It is the Sovereign LORD who helps me.
    Who will condemn me?

✠ ANCIENT WISDOM FROM TERESA OF AVILA

Let nothing trouble you.
Let nothing frighten you.
Everything passes.
God never changes.
Patience obtains all.
Whoever has God
Wants for nothing.
God alone is enough.

O God, heavenly Father, your Son Jesus Christ enjoyed rest and refreshment in the home of Mary and Martha of Bethany: Give us the will to love you, open our hearts to hear you, and strengthen our hands to serve you in others for his sake; who lives and reigns with you and the Holy Spirit, one God, now and for ever. Amen.

CHAPTER SEVEN

Thursday

On this morning, Jesus instructs Peter and John to go into the city to a mysterious "upper room." They are to have the Passover meal prepared by sunset, at the very beginning of the fourteenth of Nisan, the day when it was customary to sacrifice the Passover lamb. Passover is to be a day of celebration, but for the disciples it seems more like a funeral than a celebration, the end of an era rather than the beginning of a new one.

At sunset, Jesus and the disciples enter the city and go to a large house, where they walk upstairs and come into a spacious upper room. They see Peter and John here, finishing the preparations. This upper room will be their new home.

It is in this room that the king who rode into Jerusalem on the back of a donkey gives the disciples a glimpse of the new kingdom that, despite their doubts, is already dawning. In an astonishing display of intimacy, the king washes their feet as an example of this new politic—a hierarchy of servants rather than masters. Perhaps using the holy water for this final cleansing, Jesus wipes the disciples' feet—filthy and blistered from nearly a week of constant walking—including the feet of a nervously impatient Judas, who has one last opportunity, as Jesus tenderly strokes his feet, to repent.

They are now ready to eat the Passover. The Passover meal Peter and John prepared earlier that afternoon consists of bitter herbs with flat, stale bread. It is forbidden in the Torah to use new flour until Sunday, the second day of Unleavened Bread, when the new barley harvest will begin and fresh unleavened bread will be baked. Normally tonight's meal would have taken place tomorrow evening, after the lambs have been sacrificed at the temple.

But in this atmosphere of distress, doubt, and fear, Jesus opens their eyes to a new understanding of Passover. He is now the Passover lamb, slain to free his people. The unleavened bread and the wine are now his flesh and blood. The firstborn of the Father is laying down his life so that the firstborn of Israel—and now of Egypt and the whole world—will live. During this last supper, the old covenant is subsumed and transformed, through Christ's body and blood, into a "new covenant" in which animal sacrifice, with its regulations, is no longer needed. From now on, in the breaking of bread and the pouring of wine, every day will be Passover and Unleavened Bread, until the coming of his Father's kingdom.

This kingdom has a new mandate: Love. It is the oldest of commandments, eternally written in the human heart, but now transformed by its living embodiment. This is a love so deep that it will lay down its life for its friends. And now the eternal life of this new kingdom would be found not in financial or political security, but solely in knowing and loving God, as creatures made in his image, whose very nature and being is Truth and Love.

Since it is now two weeks after the new moon, a bright full moon shines overhead. As they leave the house, they pass along the vines that crawl up the southern wall of Jerusalem, which is lit by the moon's silvery glow. Jesus speaks to the disciples of peace in the midst of trouble, joy in the midst of grief, glory in the midst of shame, and victory in the midst of defeat—even as they are about to scatter and desert him. Now more than ever, they are confounded by his words. As the disciples near the Garden of Gethsemane at midnight, their heads aching with sorrow, one of them is still missing.

✣

MORNING

On the first day of the Festival of Unleavened Bread, when it was customary to sacrifice the Passover Lamb, Jesus sent Peter and John, saying, "Go and make preparations for us to eat the Passover."

"Where do you want us to prepare for it?" they asked.

He replied, "Go into the city, and as you enter, a man carrying a jar of water will meet you. Follow him to the house that he enters, and say to the owner of the house, 'The Teacher says: My appointed time is near. I am going to celebrate the Passover at your house. Where is my guest room, where I may eat the Passover with my disciples?' He will show you a large room upstairs, all furnished and ready. Make preparations for us there."

The disciples left, went into the city as Jesus had directed them, and found things just as he had told them. So they prepared the Passover.

✠

EVENING

When evening came, Jesus arrived with the Twelve. It was just before the Passover Festival. Jesus knew that the hour had come for him to leave this world and go to the Father. Having loved his own who were in the world, he loved them to the end.

The evening meal was in progress, and the devil had already prompted Judas, the son of Simon Iscariot, to betray Jesus. Jesus knew that the Father had put all things under his power, and that he had come from God and was returning to God; so he got up from the meal, took off his outer clothing, and wrapped a towel around his waist. After that, he poured water into a basin and began to wash his disciples' feet, drying them with the towel that was wrapped around him.

He came to Simon Peter, who said to him, "Lord, are you going to wash my feet?"

Jesus replied, "You do not realize now what I am doing, but later you will understand."

"No," said Peter, "you shall never wash my feet."

Jesus answered, "Unless I wash you, you have no part with me."

"Then, Lord," Simon Peter replied, "not just my feet but my hands and my head as well!"

Jesus answered, "Those who have had a bath need only to wash their feet; their whole body is clean. And you are clean, though not every one of you." For he knew who was going to betray him, and that was why he said not every one was clean.

When he had finished washing their feet, he put on his clothes and returned to his place. "Do you understand what I have done for you?" he asked them. "You call me 'Teacher' and 'Lord,' and rightly so, for that is what I am. Now that I, your Lord and Teacher, have washed your feet, you also should wash one another's feet. I have set you an example that you should do as I have done for you. Very truly I tell you, servants are not greater than their masters, nor are messengers greater than the one who sent them. Now that you know these things, you will be blessed if you do them.

"I am not referring to all of you; I know those I have chosen. But this is to fulfill this passage of Scripture: 'He who shared my bread has lifted up his heel against me.'

"I am telling you now before it happens, so that when it does happen you will believe that I am who I am. Very truly I tell you, whoever accepts anyone I send accepts me; and whoever accepts me accepts the one who sent me."

After he had said this, while he and his apostles were reclining at the table eating, Jesus was troubled in spirit and testified, "Very truly I tell you, one of you will betray me—one who is eating with me."

His disciples stared at one another, at a loss to know which of them he meant.

They were very sad and began to say to him one after the other, "Surely not I, Lord?"

"It is one of the Twelve," he replied. "The hand of him who is going to betray me is with mine on the table, one who has dipped his bread into the bowl with me. The Son of Man will go just as it is written about him. But woe to that man who betrays the Son of Man! It would be better for him if he had not been born." They began to question among themselves which of them it might be who would do this.

A dispute also arose among them as to which of them was considered to be greatest. Jesus said to them, "The kings of the Gentiles lord it over them; and those who exercise authority over them call themselves Benefactors. But you are not to be like that. Instead, the greatest among you should be like the youngest, and the one who rules like the one who serves. For who is greater, the one who is at the table, or the one who serves? Is it not the one who is at the table? But I am among you as one who serves.

"You are those who have stood by me in my trials. And I confer on you a kingdom, just as my Father conferred one on me, so that you may eat and drink at my table in my kingdom and sit on thrones, judging the twelve tribes of Israel."

One of them, the disciple whom Jesus loved, was reclining next to him. Simon Peter motioned to this disciple and said, "Ask him which one he means."

Leaning back against Jesus, he asked him, "Lord, who is it?"

Jesus answered, "It is the one to whom I will give this piece of bread when I have dipped it in the dish." Then, dipping the piece of bread, he gave it to Judas, the son of Simon Iscariot.

Then Judas, the one who would betray him, said, "Surely not I, Rabbi?" Jesus answered, "You have said so." As soon as Judas took the bread, Satan entered into him.

So Jesus told him, "What you are about to do, do quickly." But no one at the meal understood why Jesus said this to him. Since Judas had charge of the money, some thought Jesus was telling him to buy what was needed for the Festival, or to give something to the poor. As soon as Judas had taken the bread, he went out. And it was night.

When he was gone, Jesus said, "Now is the Son of Man glorified and God is glorified in him. If God is glorified in him, God will glorify the Son in himself, and will glorify him at once.

"My children, I will be with you only a little longer. You will look for me, and just as I told the Jews, so I tell you now: Where I am going, you cannot come.

"A new command I give you: Love one another. As I have loved you, so you must love one another. By this everyone will know that you are my disciples, if you love one another."

Simon Peter asked him, "Lord, where are you going?"

Jesus replied, "Where I am going, you cannot follow now, but you will follow later."

Peter asked, "Lord, why can't I follow you now? I will lay down my life for you."

Then Jesus answered, "Will you really lay down your life for me?"

He said to them, "I have eagerly desired to eat this Passover with you before I suffer. For I tell you, I will not eat it again until it finds fulfillment in the kingdom of God."

While they were eating, Jesus took bread, and when he had given thanks, he broke it and gave it to his disciples, saying, "Take it and eat. This is my body, which is given for you. Do this in remembrance of me."

In the same way, after the supper he took the cup, and when he had given thanks, he gave it to them, saying, "Take this, all of you, and drink from it. This is the cup of my blood, the blood of the new covenant, which is poured out for you and for many for the forgiveness of sins. Do this, whenever you drink it, in remembrance of me. For truly I tell you, I will not drink of this fruit of the vine again until that day when I drink it new with you in my Father's kingdom."

"Do not let your hearts be troubled. Trust in God; trust also in me. My Father's house has plenty of room; if that were not so, would I have told you that I am going there to prepare a place for you? And if I go and prepare a place for you, I will come back and take you to be with me that you also may be where I am. You know the way to the place where I am going."

Thomas said to him, "Lord, we don't know where you are going, so how can we know the way?"

Jesus answered, "I am the way and the truth and the life. No one comes to the Father except through me. If you really know me, you will know my Father as well. From now on, you do know him and have seen him."

Philip said, "Lord, show us the Father and that will be enough for us."

Jesus answered: "Don't you know me, Philip, even after I have been among you such a long time? Anyone who has seen me has seen the Father. How can you say, 'Show us the Father'? Don't you believe that I am in the Father, and that the Father is in me? The words I say to you I do not speak on my own authority. Rather, it is the Father, living in me, who is doing his work. Believe me when I say that I am in the Father and the Father is in me; or at least believe on the evidence of the works themselves. Very truly I tell you, all who have faith in me will do the works I have been doing, and they will do even greater things than these, because I am going to the Father. And I will do whatever you ask in my name, so that the Father may be glorified in the Son. You may ask me for anything in my name, and I will do it.

"If you love me, keep my commands. And I will ask the Father, and he will give you another advocate to help you and be with you forever—the Spirit of truth. The world cannot accept him, because it neither sees him nor knows him. But you know him, for he lives with you and will be in you. I will not leave you as orphans; I will come to you. Before long, the world will not see me anymore, but you will see me. Because I live, you also will live. On that day you will realize that I am in my Father, and you are in me, and I am in you. Whoever has my commands and keeps them is the one who loves me. Anyone who loves me will be loved by my Father, and I too will love them and show myself to them."

Then Judas (not Judas Iscariot) said, "But, Lord, why do you intend to show yourself to us and not to the world?"

Jesus replied, "Anyone who loves me will obey my teaching. My Father will love them, and we will come to them and make our home with them. Anyone who does not love me will not obey my teaching. These words you hear are not my own; they belong to the Father who sent me.

"All this I have spoken while still with you. But the Advocate, the Holy Spirit, whom the Father will send in my name, will teach you all things and will remind you of everything I have said to you.

"Peace I leave with you; my peace I give you. I do not give to you as the world gives. Do not let your hearts be troubled and do not be afraid.

"You heard me say, 'I am going away and I am coming back to you.' If you loved me, you would be glad that I am going to the Father, for the Father is greater than I. I have told you now before it happens, so that when it does happen you will believe. I will not say much more to you, for the prince of this world is coming. He has no hold over me, but he comes so that the world may learn that I love the Father and do exactly what my Father has commanded me."

Then Jesus asked them, "When I sent you without purse, bag or sandals, did you lack anything?"

"Nothing," they answered.

He said to them, "But now if you have a purse, take it, and also a bag; and if you don't have a sword, sell your cloak and buy one. It is written: 'And he was numbered with the transgressors'; and I tell you that this must be fulfilled in me. Yes, what is written about me is reaching its fulfillment."

The disciples said, "See, Lord, here are two swords."

"That is enough," he replied.

When they had sung a hymn, Jesus went out as usual to the Mount of Olives.

"Come now," he said, "let us leave." And his disciples followed him.

"I am the true vine, and my Father is the gardener. He cuts off every branch in me that bears no fruit, while every branch that does bear fruit he prunes so that it will be even more fruitful. You are already clean because of the word I have spoken to you. Remain in me, as I also remain in you. No branch can bear fruit by itself; it must remain in the vine. Neither can you bear fruit unless you remain in me.

"I am the vine; you are the branches. If you remain in me and I in you, you will bear much fruit; apart from me you can do nothing. If you do not remain in me, you are like a branch that is thrown away and withers; such branches are picked up, thrown into the fire and burned. If you remain in me and my words remain in you, ask whatever you wish, and it will be done for you. This is to my Father's glory, that you bear much fruit, showing yourselves to be my disciples.

"As the Father has loved me, so have I loved you. Now remain in my love. If you keep my commands, you will remain in my love, just as I have kept my Father's commands and remain in his love. I have told you this so that my joy may be in you and that your joy may be complete. My command is this: Love each other as I have loved you. Greater love has no one than this: to lay down one's life for one's friends. You are my friends if you do what I command. I no longer call you servants, because servants do not know their master's business. Instead, I have called you friends, for everything that I have learned from my Father I have made known to you. You did not choose me, but I chose you and appointed you so that you might go and bear fruit—fruit that will last—and so that whatever you ask in my name the Father will give you. This is my command: Love each other.

"If the world hates you, keep in mind that it hated me first. If you belonged to the world, it would love you as its own. As it is, you do not belong to the world, but I have chosen you out of the world. That is why the world hates you. Remember what I told you: 'Servants are not greater than their master.' If they persecuted me, they will persecute you also. If they obeyed my teaching, they will obey yours also. They will treat you this way because of my name, for they do not know the One who sent me. If I had not come and spoken to them, they would not be guilty of sin; but now they have no excuse for their sin. Those who hate me hate my Father as well. If I had not done among them the works no one else did, they would not be guilty of sin. As it is, they have seen, and yet they have hated both me and my Father. But this is to fulfill what is written in their Law: 'They hated me without reason.'

"When the Advocate comes, whom I will send to you from the Father—the Spirit of truth who goes out from the Father—he will testify about me. And you also must testify, for you have been with me from the beginning.

"All this I have told you so that you will not fall away. They will put you out of the synagogue; in fact, the hour is coming when those who kill you will think they are offering a service to God. They will do such things because they have not known the Father or me. I have told you this, so that when their hour comes you will remember that I warned you about them. I did not tell you this from the beginning because I was with you, but now I am going to him who sent me. None of you asks me, 'Where are you going?' Rather, you are filled with grief because I have said these things. But very truly I tell you, it is for your good that I am going away. Unless I go away, the Advocate will not come to you; but if I go, I will send him to you. When he comes, he will prove the world to be in the wrong about sin and righteousness and judgment: about sin, because people do not believe in me; about righteousness, because I am going to the Father, where you can see me no longer; and about judgment, because the prince of this world now stands condemned.

"I have much more to say to you, more than you can now bear. But when he, the Spirit of truth, comes, he will guide you into all the truth. He will not speak on his own; he will speak only what he hears, and he will tell you what is yet to come. He will glorify me because it is from me that he will receive what he will make known to you. All that belongs to the Father is mine. That is why I said the Spirit will receive from me what he will make known to you."

Jesus went on to say, "In a little while you will see me no more, and then after a little while you will see me."

At this, some of his disciples said to one another, "What does he mean by saying, 'In a little while you will see me no more, and then after a little while you will see me,' and 'Because I am going to the Father'?" They kept asking, "What does he mean by 'a little while'? We don't understand what he is saying."

Jesus saw that they wanted to ask him about this, so he said to them, "Are you asking one another what I meant when I said, 'In a little while you will see me no more, and then after a little while you will see me'? Very truly I tell you, you will weep and mourn while the world rejoices. You will grieve, but your grief will turn to joy. A woman giving birth to a child has pain because her time has come; but when her baby is born she forgets the anguish because of her joy that a child is born into the world. So with you: Now is your time of grief, but I will see you again and you will rejoice, and no one will take away your joy. In that day you will no longer ask me anything. Very truly I tell you, my Father will give you whatever you ask in my name. Until now you have not asked for anything in my name. Ask and you will receive, and your joy will be complete.

"Though I have been speaking figuratively, a time is coming when I will no longer use this kind of language but will tell you plainly about my Father. In that day you will ask in my name. I am not saying that I will ask the Father on your behalf. No, the Father himself loves you because you have loved me and have believed that I came from God. I came from the Father and entered the world; now I am leaving the world and going back to the Father."

Then Jesus' disciples said, "Now you are speaking clearly and without figures of speech. Now we can see that you know all things and that you do not even need to have anyone ask you questions. This makes us believe that you came from God."

"Do you now believe?" Jesus replied. "A time is coming and in fact has come when you will be scattered, each to your own home. You will leave me all alone. Yet I am not alone, for my Father is with me.

"I have told you these things, so that in me you may have peace. In this world you will have trouble. But take heart! I have overcome the world."

After Jesus said this, he looked toward heaven and prayed: "Father, the hour has come. Glorify your Son, that your Son may glorify you. For you granted him authority over all people that he might give eternal life to all those you have given him. Now this is eternal life: that they know you, the only true God, and Jesus Christ, whom you have sent. I have brought you glory on earth by finishing the work you gave me to do. And now, Father, glorify me in your presence with the glory I had with you before the world began.

"I have revealed you to those whom you gave me out of the world. They were yours; you gave them to me and they have obeyed your word. Now they know that everything you have given me comes from you. For I gave them the words you gave me and they accepted them. They knew with certainty that I came from you, and they believed that you sent me.

"I pray for them. I am not praying for the world, but for those you have given me, for they are yours. All I have is yours, and all you have is mine. And glory has come to me through them. I will remain in the world no longer, but they are still in the world, and I am coming to you. Holy Father, protect them by the power of your name, the name you gave me, so that they may be one as we are one. While I was with them, I protected them and kept them safe by that name you gave me. None has been lost except the one doomed to destruction so that the Scripture would be fulfilled.

"I am coming to you now, but I say these things while I am still in the world, so that they may have the full measure of my joy within them. I have given them your word and the world has hated them, for they are not of the world any more than I am of the world. My prayer is not that you take them out of the world but that you protect them from the evil one. They are not of the world, even as I am not of it. Sanctify them by the truth; your word is truth. As you sent me into the world, I have sent them into the world. For them I sanctify myself, that they too may be truly sanctified.

"My prayer is not for them alone. I pray also for those who will believe in me through their message, that all of them may be one, Father, just as you are in me and I am in you. May they also be in us so that the world may believe that you have sent me. I have given them the glory that you gave me, that they may be one as we are one—I in them and you in me—so that they may be brought to complete unity. Then the world will know that you sent me and have loved them even as you have loved me.

"Father, I want those you have given me to be with me where I am, and to see my glory, the glory you have given me because you loved me before the creation of the world.

"Righteous Father, though the world does not know you, I know you, and they know that you have sent me. I have made you known to them, and will continue to make you known in order that the love you have for me may be in them and that I myself may be in them."

✠

On the eve of the Israelites' exodus from Egypt, God gave them instructions for how to observe the Passover feast. The twelfth chapter of Exodus describes how this first Passover was observed.

✠ EXODUS 12:1–8, 11–14

The LORD said to Moses and Aaron in Egypt, "This month is to be for you the first month, the first month of your year. Tell the whole community of Israel that on the tenth day of this month each man is to take a lamb for his family, one for each household. If any household is too small for a whole lamb, they must share one with their nearest neighbor, having taken into account the number of people there are. You are to determine the amount of lamb needed in accordance with what each person will eat. The animals you choose must be year-old males without defect, and you may take them from the sheep or the goats. Take care of them until the fourteenth day of the month, when all the members of the community of Israel must slaughter them at twilight. Then they are to take some of the blood and put it on the sides and tops of the doorframes of the houses where they eat the lambs. That same night they are to eat the meat roasted over the fire, along with bitter herbs, and bread made without yeast....

"This is how you are to eat it: with your cloak tucked into your belt, your sandals on your feet and your staff in your hand. Eat it in haste; it is the LORD's Passover.

"On that same night I will pass through Egypt and strike down every firstborn of both people and animals, and I will bring judgment on all the gods of Egypt. I am the LORD. The blood will be a sign for you on the houses where you are, and when I see the blood, I will pass over you. No destructive plague will touch you when I strike Egypt.

"This is a day you are to commemorate; for the generations to come you shall celebrate it as a festival to the LORD—a lasting ordinance."

✝ ANCIENT WISDOM FROM MELITO OF SARDIS

There was much proclaimed by the prophets about the mystery of the Passover: that mystery is Christ, and to him be the glory forever and ever. Amen.

For the sake of suffering humanity he came down from heaven to earth, clothed himself in that humanity in the Virgin's womb, and was born a man. Having then a body capable of suffering, he took the pain of fallen man upon himself; he triumphed over the diseases of soul and body that were its cause, and by his Spirit, which was incapable of dying, he dealt man's destroyer, death, a fatal blow.

He was led forth like a lamb; he was slaughtered like a sheep. He ransomed us from our servitude to the world, as he had ransomed Israel from the land of Egypt; he freed us from our slavery to the devil, as he had freed Israel from the hand of Pharaoh. He sealed our souls with his own Spirit, and the members of our body with his own blood.

He is the One who covered death with shame and cast the devil into mourning, as Moses cast Pharaoh into mourning. He is the One who smote sin and robbed iniquity of offspring, as Moses robbed the Egyptians of their offspring. He is the One who brought us out of slavery into freedom, out of darkness into light, out of death into life, out of tyranny into an eternal kingdom; who made us a new priesthood, a people chosen to be his own forever. He is the Passover that is our salvation.

Almighty and everliving God, in your tender love for the human race you sent your Son our Savior Jesus Christ to take upon him our nature, and to suffer death upon the cross, giving us the example of his great humility: Mercifully grant that we may walk in the way of his suffering, and also share in his resurrection; who lives and reigns for ever and ever. Amen.

✝

CHAPTER EIGHT

Friday

Under the bright full moon, the disciples continue to follow Jesus to an olive grove at the foot of the Mount of Olives. It is in this garden that the new Adam begins to reverse the effects of the first Adam's rebellion. Amid the shadows of tortured olive tree branches, the chosen son of Eve wrestles to submit himself to God's will. Only a few days ago, Jesus had told the disciples that God could move mountains, that all things are possible to the one who believes. But now, as Jesus prays, there is no answer.

Here, alone in the garden, Jesus is overwhelmed by a sickness unto death—a mental and spiritual agony so deep it threatens to eclipse his vision of the Father's good plan. The hour of darkness has come. The weight of the world's sin lies heavy upon him: the bitterness of the betrayal by his beloved friend Judas, that one lost and confused lamb who will not be found; the faithlessness and desertion of his disciples; the suffering and cruelty he is about to endure. His priestly office will be rejected by the religious leaders, his kingship mocked by the Roman officials; he will know the humiliation of false accusation. For a brief moment in time Jesus tastes utter despair, and this is only the beginning of the cross that awaits him.

Sometime in these early morning hours of Friday, the fourteenth of Nisan, he is arrested and taken into custody. By the time he is handed over to Pilate, the busiest and most important day of the year is already underway. It is the time for preparation, when the priests must slaughter the sacrificial animals for the evening meal. On this day, long ago, Israel was to prepare hastily for their departure from Egypt. Now, centuries later, thousands of animals need to be slaughtered to provide for the enormous crowds. In order to complete the work be-

fore twilight, the priests have begun a tradition of starting the sacrifices at noon. At exactly noon, just as the shadow on the sundial becomes a thin line, the priests begin the work. Ironically, it is just at this moment that, like the penultimate plague on Egypt, darkness covers the land. The shadow on the sundial vanishes. By now the true Passover Lamb is being sacrificed.

Jesus has been taken outside the gates of the holy city and crucified naked and facing away from the temple, having been proclaimed unclean. The Roman officials have displayed him, along with two other criminals, in utter shame before the great crowds, who go in and out of the city as he bears the horrors of history and the deepest anguish of the world.

The gospels say nothing about the three hours of darkness that engulf the land as Jesus suffers crucifixion.

At three o'clock, as the altar of the temple runs with blood, Jesus dies on the cross. Puzzled by the strange signs occurring around them, the priests work hard to finish the sacrifices by sunset. The first day of Unleavened Bread is about to begin. A few of Jesus' followers remain by the cross, gazing upon the disfigured body of the one who made humankind in his image.

Only later will they come to understand that in this cross humanity's image is restored. This image had united the spiritual and earthly realms—the breath of life inhabiting the dust of the earth. From the beginning, the human person was, in its very nature, a marriage of the heavenly and the earthly. But heaven and earth were violently torn apart by our first parents' sin. Stretched out upon the cross, between heaven and earth, Jesus has reconciled the two realms in his own torn body. This was the King of the Jews—not the king the disciples were expecting, but a humble and gracious king; one whom the disciples, and eventually the whole world, would come to embrace. It was in this cross that the Tree of the Knowledge of Good and Evil, with its deadly fruit, would become the Tree of Life, with healing for all nations.

✠

MIDNIGHT

When he had finished praying, Jesus told them, "This very night you will all fall away on account of me, for it is written:

"'I will strike the shepherd,
and the sheep of the flock will be scattered.'

"But after I have risen, I will go ahead of you into Galilee."

Peter declared, "Even if all fall away on account of you, I never will."

"Simon, Simon," Jesus answered, "Satan has asked to sift all of you as wheat. But I have prayed for you, Simon, that your faith may not fail. And when you have turned back, strengthen your brothers.

"Very truly I tell you, Peter, today—yes, this very night—before the rooster crows twice you will deny three times that you know me."

But Peter insisted emphatically, "Lord, I am ready to go with you to prison. Even if I have to die with you, I will never disown you." And all the other disciples said the same.

Then Jesus and his disciples crossed the Kidron Valley. They went to a place on the other side called Gethsemane, where there was a garden, and he and his disciples went into it. On reaching the place, Jesus said to his disciples, "Sit here while I go over there and pray. Pray that you will not fall into temptation."

He took Peter and the two sons of Zebedee, James and John, along with him, and he began to be deeply distressed and troubled. Then he said to them, "My soul is overwhelmed with sorrow to the point of death. Stay here and keep watch with me."

Going a little farther, he withdrew about a stone's throw from them. He knelt down and fell with his face to the ground and prayed that if possible the hour might pass from him. "Abba, my Father," he said, "everything is possible for you. If it is possible, if you are willing, take this cup from me. Yet not what I will, but what you will." An angel from heaven appeared to him and strengthened him. And being in anguish, he prayed more earnestly, and his sweat was like drops of blood falling to the ground.

When he rose from prayer and went back to the disciples, he found them asleep, exhausted from sorrow. "Simon," he asked Peter, "are you asleep? Couldn't you men keep watch with me for one hour? Why are you sleeping? Get up. Watch and pray so that you will not fall into temptation. The spirit is willing, but the flesh is weak."

He went away for a second time and prayed the same thing, "My Father, if it is not possible for this cup to be taken away unless I drink it, may your will be done."

When he came back, he again found them sleeping, because their eyes were heavy. They did not know what to say to him. So he left them and went away once more and prayed the third time, saying the same thing.

Then he returned to the disciples and said to them, "Are you still sleeping and resting? Enough! The hour has come. Look, the Son of Man is delivered into the hands of sinners. Rise! Let us go! Here comes my betrayer!"

While he was still speaking, the man who was called Judas, one of the Twelve, arrived. Now Judas, who betrayed him, knew the place, because Jesus had often met there with his disciples. So Judas came to the garden, leading with him a large crowd: a detachment of soldiers and some officials sent from the chief priests and Pharisees, the teachers of the law, and the elders of the people. They were carrying torches and lanterns and were armed with swords and clubs.

Now the betrayer had arranged a signal with them: "The one I kiss is the man; arrest him and lead him away under guard." Going at once to Jesus, Judas said, "Greetings, Rabbi!" and kissed him. But Jesus asked him, "Judas, are you betraying the Son of Man with a kiss? Friend, do what you came for."

Jesus, knowing all that was going to happen to him, went out and asked them, "Who is it you want?"

"Jesus of Nazareth," they replied.

"I am he," Jesus said. (And Judas the traitor was standing there with them.) When Jesus said, "I am he," they drew back and fell to the ground.

Again he asked them, "Who is it you want?"

"Jesus of Nazareth," they said.

Jesus answered, "I told you that I am. If you are looking for me, then let these men go." This happened so that the words he had spoken would be fulfilled: "I have not lost one of those you gave me."

Then the men stepped forward, seized Jesus, and arrested him. When Jesus' followers saw what was going to happen, they said, "Lord, should we strike with our swords?" Then, one of Jesus' companions who was standing nearby—Simon Peter—reached for his sword, drew it out and struck the servant of the high priest, cutting off his right ear. (The servant's name was Malchus.)

But Jesus answered, "No more of this!"

"Put your sword back in its place," Jesus commanded Peter, "for all who draw the sword will die by the sword. Do you think I cannot call on my Father, and he will at once put at my disposal more than twelve legions of angels? But how then would the Scriptures be fulfilled that say it must happen in this way? Shall I not drink the cup the Father has given me?"

And he touched the man's ear and healed him.

In that hour Jesus said to the crowd—the chief priests, the officers of the temple guard, and the elders, who had come for him, "Am I leading a rebellion, that you have come out with swords and clubs to capture me? Every day I sat with you, teaching in the temple courts, and you did not arrest me. But this has all taken place that the writings of the prophets might be fulfilled. This is your hour—when darkness reigns."

Then all the disciples deserted him and fled. A young man, wearing nothing but a linen garment, was following Jesus. When they seized him, he fled naked, leaving his garment behind.

Then the detachment of soldiers with its commander and the Jewish officials bound Jesus. They led him away and took him into the house of Caiaphas, the high priest that year. All the chief priests, elders and teachers of the law had assembled there. They brought him first to Annas, who was the father-in-law of Caiaphas. Caiaphas was the one who had advised the Jewish leaders that it would be good if one man died for the people.

But Simon Peter and another disciple followed him at a distance, right up to the courtyard of the high priest. Because this disciple was known to the high priest, he went with Jesus into the high priest's courtyard, but Peter had to wait outside at the door. The other disciple, who was known to the high priest, came back, spoke to the servant girl on duty there, and brought Peter in.

It was cold, and the servants and officials stood around a fire they had kindled in the middle of the courtyard to keep warm. Peter also was standing with them, warming himself at the fire. And when the guards had sat down together, Peter sat down with them to see the outcome.

Now while Peter was sitting below in the courtyard, one of the servant girls of the high priest came by. When she saw Peter seated there, warming himself in the firelight, she looked closely at him.

"You also were with that Nazarene, Jesus of Galilee," she said. "You aren't one of this man's disciples too, are you?" she asked Peter.

But he denied it before them all. "I am not," he replied. "Woman, I don't know him. I don't know or understand what you're talking about."

Then he went out into the entryway, and the rooster crowed.

Meanwhile, the high priest questioned Jesus about his disciples and his teaching.

"I have spoken openly to the world," Jesus replied. "I always taught in synagogues or at the temple, where all the Jews come together. I said nothing in secret. Why question me? Ask those who heard me. Surely they know what I said."

When Jesus said this, one of the officials nearby slapped him in the face. "Is this the way you answer the high priest?" he demanded.

"If I said something wrong," Jesus replied, "testify as to what is wrong. But if I spoke the truth, why did you strike me?" Then Annas sent him bound to Caiaphas the high priest.

A little later, when Peter had gone out to the gateway, another servant girl saw him there. She said again to those standing around, "This fellow was one of them with Jesus of Nazareth." So they asked him, "You aren't one of his disciples, are you?"

Peter denied it again, with an oath: "Man, I am not! I don't know the man!"

The chief priests and the whole Sanhedrin were looking for false evidence against Jesus so that they could put him to death, but they did not find any. Many witnesses came forward and testified falsely against him, but their statements did not agree.

Finally two stood up, came forward and gave this false testimony against him, declaring: "We heard him say, 'I will destroy this temple of God made by human hands and in three days will build another, not made with hands.'" Yet even then their testimony did not agree.

Then the high priest stood up before them and asked Jesus, "Are you not going to answer? What is this testimony that these men are bringing against you?" But Jesus remained silent and gave no answer.

"If you are the Messiah," they said, "tell us."

Jesus answered, "If I tell you, you will not believe me, and if I asked you, you would not answer."

They all asked, "Are you then the Son of God?"

Again the high priest asked him, "Are you the Messiah, the Son of the Blessed One? I charge you under oath by the living God: Tell us if you are the Messiah, the Son of God."

"You have said so," Jesus replied. "But I say to all of you: I am. And from now on you will see the Son of Man sitting at the right hand of the Mighty One and coming on the clouds of heaven."

Then the high priest tore his clothes and said, "He has spoken blasphemy! Why do we need any more witnesses? Look, now you have heard the blasphemy from his own lips. What do you think?"

They all condemned him. "He is worthy of death," they answered.

The men who were guarding Jesus began mocking and beating him. Some spit in his face. They blindfolded him and struck him with their fists. Others slapped him and said, "Prophesy to us, Messiah! Who hit you?" And they said many other insulting things to him.

About an hour later, those standing there went up to Peter, and another asserted, "Surely you are one of them who was with him, for you are a Galilean. Your accent gives you away." One of the high priest's servants, a relative of the man whose ear Peter cut off, challenged him, "Didn't I see you with him in the garden?"

Then Peter began to call down curses. Again he denied it, and he swore to them, "Man, I don't know what you're talking about! I don't know the man!"

At that moment, just as he was speaking, the rooster crowed the second time. The Lord turned and looked straight at Peter. Then Peter remembered the word Jesus had spoken to him: "Before the rooster crows twice today, you will disown me three times." He broke down, and he went outside and wept bitterly.

✠

6 AM–9 AM

Very early in the morning, at daybreak, the council of the elders of the people, both the chief priests and teachers of the law, and the whole Sanhedrin, met together, and Jesus was led before them. They came to the decision to put Jesus to death. Then the whole assembly rose, bound him, and led him away. They took him from Caiaphas to the palace of Pilate, the Roman governor, and handed him over.

When Judas, who had betrayed him, saw that Jesus was condemned, he was seized with remorse and returned the thirty silver coins to the chief priests and the elders. "I have sinned," he said, "for I have betrayed innocent blood."

"What is that to us?" they replied. "That's your responsibility."

So Judas threw the money into the temple and left. Then he went away and hanged himself.

The chief priests picked up the coins and said, "It is against the law to put this into the treasury, since it is blood money." So they decided to use the money to buy the potter's field as a burial place for foreigners. That is why it has been called the Field of Blood to this day. Then what was spoken by Jeremiah the prophet was fulfilled: "They took the thirty silver coins, the price set on him by the people of Israel, and they used them to buy the potter's field, as the Lord commanded me."

Meanwhile Jesus stood before the governor. By now it was early morning, and to avoid ceremonial uncleanness the Jewish leaders did not enter the palace; they wanted to be able to eat the Passover. So Pilate came out to them and asked, "What charges are you bringing against this man?"

"If he were not a criminal," they replied, "we would not have handed him over to you."

Pilate said, "Take him yourselves and judge him by your own law."

"But we have no right to execute anyone," they objected. This took place to fulfill what Jesus had said about the kind of death he was going to die.

And they began to accuse him, saying, "We have found this man subverting our nation. He opposes payment of taxes to Caesar and claims to be Messiah, a king."

So Pilate asked Jesus, "Are you the king of the Jews?"

"You have said so," Jesus replied.

When he was accused of many things by the chief priests and the elders, he gave no answer. So again Pilate asked him, "Aren't you going to answer? Don't you hear the testimony they are bringing against you? See how many things they are accusing you of."

But Jesus still made no reply, not even to a single charge—to the great amazement of the governor.

Pilate then went back inside the palace, summoned Jesus and asked him, "Are you the king of the Jews?"

"Is that your own idea," Jesus asked, "or did others talk to you about me?"

"Am I a Jew?" Pilate replied. "Your own people and chief priests handed you over to me. What is it you have done?"

Jesus said, "My kingdom is not of this world. If it were, my servants would fight to prevent my arrest by the Jewish leaders. But now my kingdom is from another place."

"You are a king then!" said Pilate.

Jesus answered, "You say that I am a king. In fact, the reason I was born and came into the world is to testify to the truth. Everyone on the side of truth listens to me."

"What is truth?" Pilate asked.

With this he went out again to the Jews gathered there. Then Pilate announced to the chief priests and the crowd, "I find no basis for a charge against this man."

But they insisted, "He stirs up the people all over Judea by his teaching. He started in Galilee and has come all the way here."

On hearing this, Pilate asked if the man was a Galilean. When he learned that Jesus was under Herod's jurisdiction, he sent him to Herod, who was also in Jerusalem at that time.

When Herod saw Jesus, he was greatly pleased, because for a long time he had wanted to see him. From what he had heard about him, he hoped to see him perform some miracle. He plied him with many questions, but Jesus gave him no answer. The chief priests and the teachers of the law were standing there, vehemently accusing him. Then Herod and his soldiers ridiculed and mocked him. Dressing him in an elegant robe, they sent him back to Pilate. That day Herod and Pilate became friends—before this they had been enemies.

Pilate called together the chief priests, the rulers and the people, and said to them, "You brought me this man as one who was inciting the people to rebellion. I have examined him in your presence and have found no basis for your charges against him. Neither has Herod, for he sent him back to us; as you can see, he has done nothing to deserve death. Therefore, I will punish him and then release him. But it is your custom for me to release to you one prisoner at the time of the Passover. Do you want me to release 'the king of the Jews'?"

With one voice they shouted back, "No, not him! Away with this man! Give us Barabbas!"

Now it was the governor's custom at the Festival to release a prisoner chosen by the crowd. At that time they had a well-known prisoner whose name was Jesus Barabbas. Barabbas had been thrown into prison for taking part in an insurrection in the city, and for murder. And he was in prison with the other insurrectionists who had committed murder in the uprising. The crowd came up and asked Pilate to do for them what he usually did.

So when the crowd had gathered, Pilate asked them, "Which one do you want me to release to you: Jesus Barabbas, or Jesus who is called the Messiah, the king of the Jews?" For he knew it was out of envy that the chief priests had handed Jesus over to them.

While Pilate was sitting on the judge's seat, his wife sent him this message: "Don't have anything to do with that innocent man, for I have suffered a great deal today in a dream because of him."

Meanwhile, the chief priests and the elders were stirring up the crowd to have Pilate release Barabbas instead and to have Jesus executed.

"Which of the two do you want me to release to you?" asked the governor.

"Barabbas," they answered.

Wanting to release Jesus, Pilate appealed to them again. "What shall I do, then, with Jesus the Messiah, the one you call the king of the Jews?" Pilate asked.

They all shouted, "Crucify him!"

For the third time he spoke to them: "Why? What crime has this man committed? I have found in him no grounds for the death penalty. Therefore I will have him punished and then release him."

But they kept shouting, "Crucify him! Crucify him!"

Wanting to satisfy the crowd, Pilate released Barabbas to them—the man who had been thrown into prison for insurrection and murder, the one they asked for.

Then Pilate took Jesus and had him flogged.

After he was flogged, the governor's soldiers led Jesus away into the palace (that is, the Praetorium) and called together the whole company of soldiers around him. They stripped him and clothed him in a scarlet robe, then twisted together a crown of thorns and set it on his head. They put a staff in his right hand as a scepter, then knelt in front of him and mocked him. "Hail, king of the Jews!" they called out. Then they took the staff and struck him on the head again and again; and they spit on him and slapped him in the face. Falling on their knees, they paid homage to him.

Once more Pilate came out and said to the Jews, "Look, I am bringing him out to you to let you know that I find no basis for a charge against him." When Jesus came out wearing the crown of thorns and the purple robe, Pilate said to them, "Here is the man!"
As soon as the chief priests and their officials saw him, they shouted, "Crucify! Crucify!"
But Pilate answered, "You take him and crucify him. As for me, I find no basis for a charge against him."
They insisted, "We have a law, and according to that law he must die, because he claimed to be the Son of God."

When Pilate heard this, he was even more afraid, and he went back inside the palace. "Where do you come from?" he asked Jesus, but Jesus gave him no answer. "Do you refuse to speak to me?" Pilate said. "Don't you realize I have power either to free you or to crucify you?"
Jesus answered, "You would have no power over me if it were not given to you from above. Therefore the one who handed me over to you is guilty of a greater sin."
From then on, Pilate tried to set Jesus free, but the Jewish leaders kept shouting, "If you let this man go, you are no friend of Caesar. Anyone who claims to be a king opposes Caesar."

✠

9 AM–12 NOON

When Pilate heard this, he brought Jesus out and sat down on the
judge's seat at a place known as the Stone Pavement (which in
Aramaic is Gabbatha). It was the day of Preparation of the
Passover; it was about noon.

"Here is your king," Pilate said to the Jews.

But they shouted, "Take him away! Take him away! Crucify
him!"

"Shall I crucify your king?" Pilate asked.

"We have no king but Caesar," the chief priests answered.

With loud shouts they insistently demanded that he be crucified.
They shouted all the louder, "Crucify him!" and their shouts
prevailed.

When Pilate saw that he was getting nowhere, but that instead
an uproar was starting, he finally decided to grant their demand. He
took water and washed his hands in front of the crowd. "I am
innocent of this man's blood," he said. "It is your responsibility!"

All the people answered, "His blood is on us and on our
children!"

Pilate surrendered Jesus to their will and handed him over to
them to be crucified.

So the soldiers took charge of Jesus. They took off the purple
robe and put his own clothes on him. Then, carrying his own cross,
they led him away to crucify him.

As they were going out, they met a certain man from Cyrene,
named Simon, the father of Alexander and Rufus, who was passing
by on his way in from the country. And they put the cross on him
and forced him to carry it behind Jesus.

A large number of people followed him, including women who
mourned and wailed for him. Jesus turned and said to them,
"Daughters of Jerusalem, do not weep for me; weep for yourselves
and for your children. For the time will come when you will say,
'Blessed are the childless women, the wombs that never bore and
the breasts that never nursed!' Then

> "'they will say to the mountains, "Fall on us!"
> and to the hills, "Cover us!"'"

"For if people do these things when the tree is green, what will happen when it is dry?"

Two other men, both criminals, were also led out with him to be executed.

They brought Jesus out to a place called Golgotha (which means The Place of the Skull in Aramaic). There they offered Jesus wine to drink, mixed with myrrh; but after tasting it, he refused to drink it. And they crucified him there. The two rebels were crucified along with him—one on his right, the other one on his left, and Jesus in the middle. Jesus said, "Father, forgive them, for they do not know what they are doing." It was nine in the morning when they crucified him.

When the soldiers had crucified Jesus, they took his clothes, dividing them into four shares, one for each of them, with the undergarment remaining. This garment was seamless, woven in one piece from top to bottom.

"Let's not tear it," they said to one another. "Let's decide by lot who will get it."

This happened that the scripture might be fulfilled which said,

"They divided my clothing among them
    and cast lots for my garments."

So this is what the soldiers did. They cast lots to see what each would get. And sitting down, they kept watch over him there.

Pilate had a written notice of the charge against him prepared. They fastened it to the cross, placing it above his head. It read:

THIS IS
JESUS OF NAZARETH,
THE KING OF THE JEWS.

Many of the Jews read this sign, for the place where Jesus was crucified was near the city, and the sign was written in Aramaic, Latin and Greek. The chief priests of the Jews protested to Pilate, "Do not write 'The king of the Jews,' but that this man claimed to be king of the Jews."

Pilate answered, "What I have written, I have written."

The people stood watching, and those who passed by hurled insults at him, shaking their heads and saying,

"So! You who are going to destroy the temple and build it in three days, save yourself! Come down from the cross if you are the Son of God!"

In the same way the chief priests, the teachers of the law and the elders mocked him among themselves:

"He saved others," they said, "but he can't save himself! Let him save himself if he is God's Messiah, the Chosen One."

"He's the king of Israel! Let this Messiah, this king of Israel, come down now from the cross, that we may see and believe in him."

"He trusts in God. Let God rescue him now if he wants him, for he said, 'I am the Son of God.'"

The soldiers also came up to him and mocked him. They offered him wine vinegar and said, "If you are the king of the Jews, save yourself."

In the same way one of the criminals who hung there with him hurled insults at him: "Aren't you the Messiah? Save yourself and us!"

But the other criminal rebuked him. "Don't you fear God," he said, "since you are under the same sentence? We are punished justly, for we are getting what our deeds deserve. But this man has done nothing wrong."

Then he said, "Jesus, remember me when you come into your kingdom."

Jesus answered him, "Truly I tell you, today you will be with me in paradise."

Near the cross of Jesus stood his mother, his mother's sister, Mary the wife of Clopas, and Mary Magdalene. When Jesus saw his mother there, and the disciple whom he loved standing nearby, he said to her, "Woman, here is your son," and to the disciple, "Here is your mother." From that time on, this disciple took her into his home.

✠

12 NOON–3 PM

It was now about noon, and darkness came over the whole land until three in the afternoon, for the sun stopped shining.

✛

3 PM–6 PM

Later, at about three in the afternoon Jesus cried out in a loud voice, "Eloi, Eloi, lema sabachthani?"—which means, "My God, my God, why have you forsaken me?"

When some of those standing near heard this, they said, "Listen, he's calling Elijah."

Knowing that everything had now been finished, and so that scripture would be fulfilled, Jesus said, "I am thirsty."

A jar of wine vinegar was there, so immediately one of them ran and got a sponge. He soaked the sponge with wine vinegar, put the sponge on a stalk of the hyssop plant, and offered it to Jesus to drink, lifting it to Jesus' lips. The rest said, "Now leave him alone. Let's see if Elijah comes to take him down."

When he had received the drink, Jesus said, "It is finished."

Jesus cried out again with a loud voice, "Father, into your hands I commit my spirit."

When he had said this, Jesus breathed his last. And he bowed his head and gave up his spirit.

At that moment the curtain of the temple was torn in two from top to bottom. The earth shook, the rocks split, and the tombs broke open. The bodies of many holy people who had died were raised to life. They came out of the tombs after Jesus' resurrection and went into the holy city and appeared to many people.

And when the centurion, who stood there in front of Jesus, and those with him who were guarding Jesus, saw how he died—the earthquake and all that had happened—they were terrified. And he praised God and exclaimed, "Surely this righteous man was the Son of God!" When all the people who had gathered to witness this sight saw what took place, they beat their breasts and went away.

But all those who knew him, including the many women who had followed him from Galilee, stood at a distance, watching these things. Among them were Mary Magdalene, Mary the mother of James the younger and of Joses, Salome, and the mother of Zebedee's sons. In Galilee these women had followed Jesus and cared for his needs. Many other women who had come up with him to Jerusalem were also there.

Now it was the day of Preparation, and the next day was to be a special Sabbath. Because the Jewish leaders did not want the bodies left on the crosses during the Sabbath, they asked Pilate to have the legs broken and the bodies taken down. The soldiers therefore came and broke the legs of the first man who had been crucified with Jesus, and then those of the other. But when they came to Jesus and found that he was already dead, they did not break his legs. Instead, one of the soldiers pierced Jesus' side with a spear, bringing a sudden flow of blood and water.

The man who saw it has given testimony, and his testimony is true. He knows that he tells the truth, and he testifies so that you also may believe. These things happened so that the scripture would be fulfilled: "Not one of his bones will be broken," and, as another scripture says, "They will look on the one they have pierced."

Later, as evening approached, there came a rich man from the Judean town of Arimathea, named Joseph, who was himself waiting for the kingdom of God. He was a prominent member of the Council, a good and upright man, who had not consented to their decision and action. Now Joseph had himself become a disciple of Jesus, but secretly because he feared the Jewish leaders.

Going boldly to Pilate, he asked for the body of Jesus. Pilate was surprised to hear that he was already dead. Summoning the centurion, he asked him if Jesus had already died. When he learned from the centurion that it was so, Pilate ordered that the body be given to Joseph.

So Joseph bought some linen cloth and, with Pilate's permission, came to take the body away. He was accompanied by Nicodemus, the man who earlier had visited Jesus at night. Nicodemus brought a mixture of myrrh and aloes, about seventy-five pounds.

After taking down Jesus' body, the two of them wrapped it, with the spices, in the clean strips of linen cloth. This was in accordance with Jewish burial customs.

At the place where Jesus was crucified, there was a garden. And in the garden was Joseph's own tomb, which he had cut out of the rock—a new tomb in which no one had ever been laid. It was the Jewish Day of Preparation (that is, the day before the Sabbath) and the Sabbath was about to begin. Since the tomb was nearby, they laid Jesus there. Then he rolled a big stone against the entrance of the tomb and went away.

The women who had come with Jesus from Galilee—Mary Magdalene and the other Mary, the mother of Joses—followed Joseph. They were sitting there opposite the tomb, and they saw how his body was laid in it.

Then they went home and prepared spices and perfumes. But they rested on the Sabbath in obedience to the commandment.

The prophet Isaiah's ode to the suffering servant is one of the most compelling prophecies in the entire Bible, and early Christian interpretation applied these verses to Jesus as one who suffered unjustly and, through his suffering, heals and redeems the world.

✝ ISAIAH 53:3–9

He was despised and rejected by others,
    a man of suffering, and familiar with pain.

Like one from whom people hide their faces
    he was despised, and we held him in low esteem.

Surely he took up our pain
    and bore our suffering,
yet we considered him punished by God,
    stricken by him, and afflicted.

But he was pierced for our transgressions,
    he was crushed for our iniquities;
the punishment that brought us peace was on him,
    and by his wounds we are healed.

We all, like sheep, have gone astray,
    each of us has turned to our own way;
and the LORD has laid on him
    the iniquity of us all.

He was oppressed and afflicted,
    yet he did not open his mouth;
he was led like a lamb to the slaughter,
    and as a sheep before its shearers is silent,
    so he did not open his mouth.

By oppression and judgment he was taken away.
  Yet who of his generation protested?

For he was cut off from the land of the living;
  for the transgression of my people he was punished.

He was assigned a grave with the wicked,
  and with the rich in his death,
though he had done no violence,
  nor was any deceit in his mouth.

 Ancient Wisdom from John Chrysostom

If you desire further proof of the power of this blood, remember where it came from, how it ran down from the cross, flowing from the Master's side. The gospel records that when Christ was dead, but still hung on the cross, a soldier came and pierced his side with a lance and immediately there poured out water and blood. Now the water was a symbol of baptism and the blood, of the holy eucharist. The soldier pierced the Lord's side, he breached the wall of the sacred temple, and I have found the treasure and made it my own.

Almighty God, whose most dear Son went not up to joy but first he suffered pain, and entered not into glory before he was crucified: Mercifully grant that we, walking in the way of the cross, may find it none other than the way of life and peace; through Jesus Christ your Son our Lord. Amen.

$$\text{⁺⊹⁺}$$

CHAPTER NINE

Saturday

Last night, after sunset, the disciples had scattered—some perhaps back to Bethany, others locking themselves inside the upper room. Outside, numerous small fires burned in the soft glow of twilight. Smoke from the Passover sacrifices made the moon look red as it rose over the Mount of Olives. The stars, one by one, began to shine. The pilgrims, many of whom were unaware of what had happened to the rabbi teaching in the temple courts just days ago, began to eat the unleavened bread and the meat roasted with bitter herbs.

"What does all this mean?" the little children would ask. The parents gently responded: "It was this very night that the Israelites took the blood of the Passover lambs and put it on the doorposts of their houses with a hyssop branch. Then they roasted the meat with bitter herbs to symbolize the bitterness of their years of slavery in Egypt. They locked themselves in their houses and didn't dare go outside until the next morning; the final plague was about to come upon Egypt. At midnight they huddled together as the angel of God struck the land. But when the angel saw the blood on the Israelite houses, he passed over them. When morning came, the Israelites cracked opened the doors and looked outside. They were free to go." With the ancient story replaying in their minds, the children went to sleep and imagined themselves, long ago, following a bright cloud wherever it went.

The disciples awake, stunned. It is Saturday, the fifteenth day of Nisan. In obedience to the Torah, the disciples spend the first day of Unleavened Bread remembering their freedom from slavery. There is a tradition, in keeping with this day of freedom, that Pilate must release a Jewish prisoner each year on the eve of Passover. This year it

*had come down to two: Yeshua Bar-Abbas ("Jesus, son of the father")
or Yeshua, the only begotten Son of the Father. One had to die to set
the other free. This year it was Bar-Abbas who went free.*

*As the bewildered disciples mourn the death of the Messiah, their
hopes dashed, they wait in the quiet and calm of this Sabbath day,
when God rested from all his work. Their Lord lies in a sealed and
dark tomb, cut off from his own creation, hidden in a womb of rock
and earth.*

✠

MIDDAY

The next day, the one after Preparation Day, the chief priests and
the Pharisees went to Pilate. "Sir," they said, "we remember that
while he was still alive that deceiver said, 'After three days I will rise
again.' So give the order for the tomb to be made secure until the
third day. Otherwise, his disciples may come and steal the body and
tell the people that he has been raised from the dead. This last
deception will be worse than the first."

"Take a guard," Pilate answered. "Go, make the tomb as secure
as you know how." So they went and made the tomb secure by
putting a seal on the stone and posting the guard.

✠

EVENING

When the Sabbath was over, Mary Magdalene, Mary the mother of
James, and Salome bought spices so that they might go to anoint
Jesus' body.

*Many churches hold a Saturday Easter vigil service in which Christ's
resurrection is observed at midnight, and it is common at this service
to read through certain Old Testament passages that Christians believe to prefigure the work of Christ. These readings start with the
creation account, signifying that we are about to enter into a new creation through Christ's resurrection.*

Two of the most memorable stories in the Bible follow the creation account, the story of Abraham and Isaac and the account of Israel's escape from Egypt. Just as Isaac ascended the hill of Moriah with the heavy burden of the sacrificial wood on his back, so too would Jesus ascend the hill of Golgotha with the wood of the cross on his back. The Israelites' crossing from death to life, through the waters of the Red Sea, occurred at sunrise just days after the Passover, when their freedom had been bought by the blood of a firstborn lamb. These passages are summed up in the apostle Paul's discourse on the meaning of baptism, by which we enter into Christ's resurrection. And so we are drawn into the deep darkness of the tomb of Christ, where we will witness the brilliant flash of light that changed the world forever.

✠ GENESIS 22:1–2, 4, 6–8

Some time later God tested Abraham. He said to him, "Abraham!"

"Here I am," he replied.

Then God said, "Take your son, your only son, whom you love—Isaac—and go to the region of Moriah. Sacrifice him there as a burnt offering on a mountain I will show you."

On the third day Abraham looked up and saw the place in the distance.

Abraham took the wood for the burnt offering and placed it on his son Isaac, and he himself carried the fire and the knife. As the two of them went on together, Isaac spoke up and said to his father Abraham, "Father?"

"Yes, my son?" Abraham replied.

"The fire and wood are here," Isaac said, "but where is the lamb for the burnt offering?"

Abraham answered, "God himself will provide the lamb for the burnt offering, my son."

✠ EXODUS 14:15A, 16, 19–27A, 29–30A

The LORD said to Moses, "Raise your staff and stretch out your hand over the sea to divide the water so that the Israelites can go through the sea on dry ground."

Then the angel of God, who had been traveling in front of Israel's army, withdrew and went behind them. The pillar of cloud also moved from in front and stood behind them, coming between the armies of Egypt and Israel. Throughout the night the cloud brought darkness to the one side and light to the other side; so neither went near the other all night long.

Then Moses stretched out his hand over the sea, and all that night the LORD drove the sea back with a strong east wind and turned it into dry land. The waters were divided, and the Israelites went through the sea on dry ground, with a wall of water on their right and on their left.

The Egyptians pursued them, and all Pharaoh's horses and chariots and horsemen followed them into the sea. During the last watch of the night the LORD looked down from the pillar of fire and cloud at the Egyptian army and threw it into confusion. He jammed the wheels of their chariots so that they had difficulty driving. And the Egyptians said, "Let's get away from the Israelites! The LORD is fighting for them against Egypt."

Then the LORD said to Moses, "Stretch out your hand over the sea so that the waters may flow back over the Egyptians and their chariots and horsemen." Moses stretched out his hand over the sea, and at daybreak the sea went back to its place.

But the Israelites went through the sea on dry ground, with a wall of water on their right and on their left. That day the LORD saved Israel from the hands of the Egyptians.

✟ ROMANS 6:3–11

Don't you know that all of us who were baptized into Christ Jesus were baptized into his death? We were therefore buried with him through baptism into death in order that, just as Christ was raised from the dead through the glory of the Father, we too may live a new life.

If we have been united with him in a death like his, we will certainly also be united with him in a resurrection like his. For we know that our old self was crucified with him so that the body ruled by sin might be done away with, that we should no longer be slaves to sin—because anyone who has died has been set free from sin.

Now if we died with Christ, we believe that we will also live with him. For we know that since Christ was raised from the dead, he cannot die again; death no longer has mastery over him. The death he died, he died to sin once for all; but the life he lives, he lives to God.

In the same way, count yourselves dead to sin but alive to God in Christ Jesus.

ANCIENT WISDOM FROM AN UNKNOWN PREACHER

Today a great silence reigns on earth, a great silence and a great stillness. A great silence because the King is asleep. The earth trembled and is still because God has fallen asleep in the flesh and he has raised up all who have slept ever since the world began....

He has gone to search for Adam, our first father, as for a lost sheep. Greatly desiring to visit those who live in darkness and in the shadow of death, he has gone to free from sorrow Adam in his bonds and Eve, captive with him—He who is both their God and the son of Eve....

"I am your God, who for your sake have become your son....I order you, O sleeper, to awake. I did not create you to be a prisoner in hell. Rise from the dead, for I am the life of the dead."

O God, your blessed Son was laid in a tomb in a garden, and rested on the Sabbath day: Grant that we who have been buried with him in the waters of baptism may find our perfect rest in his eternal and glorious kingdom; where he lives and reigns for ever and ever. Amen.

CHAPTER TEN

Easter Sunday

For Christians, Easter Day is a day of celebration in remembrance of Christ's victory over death, a day that marks the beginning of eternal life. But for the disciples this is a day of conflicting and overwhelming emotions, ranging from ecstatic joy to sheer terror. His appearance after such a violent death is a dizzying realization, as if the whole world has been turned upside down and inside out.

This second day of Unleavened Bread, the sixteenth of Nisan, marks the beginning of the barley harvest, the first crop of the year. Sometime this morning, in fulfillment of the Torah, a sickle is put to a stand of newly ripened barley. These "firstfruits" are then brought to the temple, where the priests present them before God. The harvest has begun, and it will continue for seven weeks. On the fiftieth day, Pentecost, the barley harvest will conclude and the wheat harvest will begin. Today's firstfruits represent the first produce to come out of the dormant, hard winter soil and into the fresh spring air, bursting with new life.

This afternoon, Jesus meets two of his friends as they walk to a village called Emmaus. Not recognizing him, they relate to him the recent events in Jerusalem. When they reach the village, Jesus sits down to eat with them. He breaks fresh, newly baked bread, and the two suddenly recognize him.

Christ's resurrection will set the church—that family of God founded by the apostles—in motion. But the eleven apostles are the last to believe. The women who go to Jesus' grave and witness the resurrection are the first. Though Jesus will later instruct Peter to feed and guide his flock, it is Mary Magdalene's witness that gives birth to Christianity.

☦

EARLY MORNING

At the dawning of the first day of the week, very early in the morning, while it was still dark, the women took the spices they had prepared and went to look at the tomb.

There was a violent earthquake, for an angel of the Lord came down from heaven and, going to the tomb, rolled back the stone and sat on it. His appearance was like lightning, and his clothes were white as snow. The guards were so afraid of him that they shook and became like dead men.

Just after sunrise, as the women were on their way to the tomb, they asked each other, "Who will roll the stone away from the entrance of the tomb?" When they looked up, they saw that the stone, which was very large, had been rolled away. But when they entered the tomb, they did not find the body of the Lord Jesus.

So Mary Magdalene came running to Simon Peter and the other disciple, the one Jesus loved, and said, "They have taken the Lord out of the tomb, and we don't know where they have put him!" So Peter and the other disciple got up and started running for the tomb.

While the women were wondering about this, they suddenly saw two young men dressed in white robes that gleamed like lightning standing beside them, and they were alarmed. In their fright, the women bowed down with their faces to the ground, but the men said to them, "Why do you look for the living among the dead?"

The angel sitting on the right side said to the women, "Do not be afraid, for I know that you are looking for Jesus the Nazarene, who was crucified. He is not here; he has risen, just as he said! Remember how he told you, while he was still with you in Galilee: 'The Son of Man must be delivered into the hands of sinful men, be crucified and on the third day be raised again.'" Then they remembered his words.

"Come and see the place where they laid him. Then go quickly and tell his disciples and Peter: 'He has risen from the dead and is going ahead of you into Galilee. There you will see him, just as he told you.'"

So the women hurried out and fled from the tomb, trembling and bewildered, afraid, yet filled with joy. They said nothing to anyone, because they were afraid.

Meanwhile, Peter and the other disciple were both running for the tomb, but the other disciple outran Peter and reached the tomb first. He bent over and looked in at the strips of linen lying there but did not go in.

Then Simon Peter, who was behind him, arrived and went straight into the tomb. He saw the strips of linen lying there by themselves, as well as the cloth that had been wrapped around Jesus' head. The cloth was still lying in its place, separate from the linen.

Finally the other disciple, who had reached the tomb first, also went inside. He saw and believed. (They still did not understand from Scripture that Jesus had to rise from the dead.) Then the disciples went back to where they were staying.

As Peter went away, he wondered to himself what had happened.

Now Mary stood outside the tomb crying. As she wept, she bent over to look into the tomb and saw two angels in white, seated where Jesus' body had been, one at the head and the other at the foot.

They asked her, "Woman, why are you crying?"

"They have taken my Lord away," she said, "and I don't know where they have put him." At this, she turned around and saw Jesus standing there, but she did not realize that it was Jesus.

"Woman," he asked her, "Why are you crying? Who is it you are looking for?"

Thinking he was the gardener, she said, "Sir, if you have carried him away, tell me where you have put him, and I will get him."

Jesus said to her, "Mary."

She turned toward him and cried out in Aramaic, "Rabboni!" (which means "Teacher").

Jesus said, "Do not hold on to me, for I have not yet ascended to the Father. Go instead to my brothers and tell them, 'I am ascending to my Father and your Father, to my God and your God.'"

Later, as the women ran to tell his disciples, Jesus suddenly met them. "Greetings," he said. They came to him, clasped his feet and worshiped him. Then Jesus said to them, "Do not be afraid. Go and tell my brothers to go to Galilee; there they will see me."

While the women were on their way, some of the guards went into the city and reported to the chief priests everything that had happened. When the chief priests had met with the elders and devised a plan, they gave the soldiers a large sum of money, telling them, "You are to say, 'His disciples came during the night and stole him away while we were asleep.' If this report gets to the governor, we will satisfy him and keep you out of trouble." So the soldiers took the money and did as they were instructed. And this story has been widely circulated among the Jews to this very day.

When the women came back from the tomb, they told all these things to the Eleven who had been with him, and to all the others who were mourning and weeping. It was Mary Magdalene, Joanna, Mary the mother of James, and the others with them who told this to the apostles.

Jesus appeared first to Mary Magdalene, out of whom he had driven seven demons. So Mary told the disciples the news: "I have seen the Lord!" And she told them what he had said to her. But when they heard that Jesus was alive and that they had seen him, they did not believe the women, because their words seemed to them like nonsense.

✠

AFTERNOON

Now that same day two of them were walking in the country. They were going to a village called Emmaus, about seven miles from Jerusalem, and they were talking with each other about everything that had happened. As they talked and discussed these things with each other, Jesus himself came up and walked along with them; but they were kept from recognizing him for he appeared to them in a different form.

He asked them, "What are you discussing together as you walk along?"

They stood still, their faces downcast. One of them, named Cleopas, asked him, "Are you only a visitor to Jerusalem and do not know the things that have happened there in these days?"

"What things?" he asked.

"About Jesus of Nazareth," they replied. "He was a prophet, powerful in word and deed before God and all the people. The chief priests and our rulers handed him over to be sentenced to death, and they crucified him; but we had hoped that he was the one who was going to redeem Israel. And what is more, it is the third day since all this took place. In addition, some of our women amazed us. They went to the tomb early this morning but didn't find his body. They came and told us that they had seen a vision of angels, who said he was alive. Then some of our companions went to the tomb and found it just as the women had said, but him they did not see."

He said to them, "How foolish you are, and how slow to believe all that the prophets have spoken! Did not the Messiah have to suffer these things and then enter his glory?" And beginning with Moses and all the Prophets, he explained to them what was said in all the Scriptures concerning himself.

✠

LATE AFTERNOON

As they approached the village to which they were going, Jesus continued on as if he were going farther. But they urged him strongly, "Stay with us, for it is nearly evening; the day is almost over." So he went in to stay with them.

When he was at the table with them, he took bread, gave thanks, broke it and began to give it to them. Then their eyes were opened and they recognized him, and he disappeared from their sight. They asked each other, "Were not our hearts burning within us while he talked with us on the road and opened the Scriptures to us?"

They got up and returned at once to Jerusalem.

✠

EVENING

On the evening of that first day of the week, they found the Eleven and the rest of those with them, assembled together, with the doors locked for fear of the Jewish leaders. And some were saying, "It is true! The Lord has risen and has appeared to Simon." Then the two reported what had happened on the way, and how Jesus was recognized by them when he broke the bread. But they did not believe them either.

While they were still talking about this, Jesus himself appeared to the Eleven as they were eating. He came and stood among them and said, "Peace be with you!"

They were startled and frightened, thinking they saw a ghost. And he rebuked them for their lack of faith and their stubborn refusal to believe those who had seen him after he had risen. He said to them, "Why are you troubled, and why do doubts arise in your minds? Look at my hands and my feet. It is I myself! Touch me and see; a ghost does not have flesh and bones, as you see I have."

When he had said this, he showed them his hands and feet, and his side. The disciples were overjoyed when they saw the Lord.

And while they still did not believe it because of joy and amazement, he asked them, "Do you have anything here to eat?" They gave him a piece of broiled fish, and he took it and ate it in their presence.

He said to them, "This is what I told you while I was still with you: Everything must be fulfilled that is written about me in the Law of Moses, the Prophets and the Psalms."

Then he opened their minds so they could understand the Scriptures. He told them, "This is what is written: The Messiah will suffer and rise from the dead on the third day, and repentance for the forgiveness of sins will be preached in his name to all nations, beginning at Jerusalem. You are witnesses of these things.

"Go into all the world and preach the good news to all creation. Whoever believes and is baptized will be saved, but whoever does not believe will be condemned. And these signs will accompany those who believe: In my name they will drive out demons; they will speak in new tongues; they will pick up snakes with their hands; and when they drink deadly poison, it will not hurt them at all; they will place their hands on sick people, and they will get well."

Again Jesus said to them, "Peace be with you! As the Father has sent me, I am sending you." And with that he breathed on them and said, "Receive the Holy Spirit. If you forgive the sins of anyone, their sins are forgiven; if you do not forgive them, they are not forgiven."

NIGHT

Now Thomas (called Didymus), one of the Twelve, was not with the disciples when Jesus came. So the other disciples told him, "We have seen the Lord!"

But he said to them, "Unless I see the nail marks in his hands and put my finger where the nails were, and put my hand into his side, I will not believe."

In his letter to the Colossians, Paul proclaims the risen Savior, and the spiritual and physical transformation God brings when we ourselves participate in Christ's death and resurrection.

✠ COLOSSIANS 3:1–4

Since, then, you have been raised with Christ, set your hearts on things above, where Christ is seated at the right hand of God. Set your minds on things above, not on earthly things. For you died, and your life is now hidden with Christ in God. When Christ, who is your life, appears, then you also will appear with him in glory.

✠ ANCIENT WISDOM FROM MAXIMUS OF TURIN

Christ is risen! He has burst open the gates of hell and let the dead go free; he has renewed the earth through the members of his Church now born again in baptism, and has made it blossom afresh with men brought back to life. His Holy Spirit has unlocked the doors of heaven, which stand wide open to receive those who rise up from the earth. Because of Christ's resurrection the thief ascends to paradise, the bodies of the blessed enter the holy city, and the dead are restored to the company of the living. There is an upward movement in the whole of creation, each element raising itself to something higher. We see hell restoring its victims to the upper regions, earth sending its buried dead to heaven, and heaven presenting the new arrivals to the Lord. In one and the same movement, our Savior's passion raises men from the depths, lifts them up from the earth, and sets them in the heights.

Christ is risen. His rising brings to life the dead, forgiveness to sinners, and glory to the saints. And so David the prophet summons all creation to join in celebrating the Easter festival: *Rejoice and be glad,* he cries, *on this day which the Lord has made.*

O God, who by the glorious resurrection of your Son Jesus Christ destroyed death and brought life and immortality to light: Grant that we, who have been raised with him, may abide in his presence and rejoice in the hope of eternal glory; through Jesus Christ our Lord, to whom, with you and the Holy Spirit, be dominion and praise for ever and ever. Amen.

CHAPTER ELEVEN

Ascension

The Easter story does not end with Christ's resurrection, for the story is not complete without Jesus' ascension into heaven and his sending of the Holy Spirit on the day of Pentecost. Jesus' passion makes little sense divorced from its main end—the gathering of a community formed in God's love and power to share in the divine life.

The gospels give us just a few vivid snapshots of what happened during those mysterious forty days before the ascension, in which Jesus appeared to his disciples—and not only to them. The apostle Paul would later report in his first letter to the Corinthians that Jesus "appeared to more than five hundred of the brothers and sisters at the same time, most of whom are still living, though some have fallen asleep." John concludes his gospel with a coda that expresses the bittersweet emotions the disciples must have felt after Jesus ascended to the Father: "Jesus did many other miraculous signs in the presence of his disciples, which are not recorded in this book. If every one of them were written down, I suppose that even the whole world would not have room for the books that would be written. But these are written that you may believe that Jesus is the Messiah, the Son of God, and that by believing you may have life in his name."

On Friday, the twenty-first day of Nisan, exactly one week after Jesus had been crucified, the disciples celebrated the seventh and last day of Unleavened Bread. Like the first day, it was a solemn day of rest and of worship. But unlike that first day of Unleavened Bread, this was a day of great rejoicing for the disciples, even if the miraculous events of this year's festival hadn't quite sunk in. Toward evening everyone prepared for the oncoming Sabbath, which made for a holiday one day longer than usual. In a few days, the hundreds of thou-

sands of pilgrims in and around Jerusalem will say goodbye to their hosts, relatives, and friends, and leave for home. At sunset, the disciples remembered that this was the night that Israel crossed through the Red Sea and made it to the desert of Sinai. The Israelites no longer had to eat unleavened bread and bitter herbs. From now on, they would eat the bread of heaven.

When the gospel narrative resumes after Easter Sunday, we find that a week has passed since the risen Jesus appeared to his disciples in the upper room. Now they are gathered there again. It is Sunday, the twenty-third day of Nisan. The disciples are excited, perhaps confused, yet certain that they have seen him. But where has he been, and where is he now?

After his suffering, he presented himself to them and gave many convincing proofs that he was alive. He appeared to them over a period of forty days and spoke about the kingdom of God.

A week after he first appeared to them, the disciples were in the house again, and Thomas was with them. Though the doors were locked, Jesus came and stood among them and said, "Peace be with you!" Then he said to Thomas, "Put your finger here; see my hands. Reach out your hand and put it into my side. Stop doubting and believe."

Thomas said to him, "My Lord and my God!"

Then Jesus told him, "Because you have seen me, you have believed; blessed are those who have not seen and yet have believed."

Afterward Jesus appeared again to his disciples, by the Sea of Tiberias. It happened this way: Simon Peter, Thomas (called Didymus), Nathanael from Cana in Galilee, the sons of Zebedee, and two other disciples were together. "I'm going out to fish," Simon Peter told them, and they said, "We'll go with you." So they went out and got into the boat, but that night they caught nothing.

Early in the morning, Jesus stood on the shore, but the disciples did not realize that it was Jesus.

He called out to them, "Friends, haven't you any fish?"

"No," they answered.

He said, "Throw your net on the right side of the boat and you will find some." When they did, they were unable to haul the net in because of the large number of fish.

Then the disciple whom Jesus loved said to Peter, "It is the Lord!" As soon as Simon Peter heard him say, "It is the Lord," he wrapped his outer garment around him (for he had taken it off) and jumped into the water. The other disciples followed in the boat, towing the net full of fish, for they were not far from shore, about a hundred yards. When they landed, they saw a fire of burning coals there with fish on it, and some bread.

Jesus said to them, "Bring some of the fish you have just caught."

Simon Peter climbed aboard and dragged the net ashore. It was full of large fish, 153, but even with so many the net was not torn. Jesus said to them, "Come and have breakfast." None of the disciples dared ask him, "Who are you?" They knew it was the Lord. Jesus came, took the bread and gave it to them, and did the same with the fish. This was now the third time Jesus appeared to his disciples after he was raised from the dead.

When they had finished eating, Jesus said to Simon Peter, "Simon son of John, do you love me more than these?"

"Yes, Lord," he said, "you know that I love you."

Jesus said, "Feed my lambs."

Again Jesus said, "Simon son of John, do you love me?"

He answered, "Yes, Lord, you know that I love you."

Jesus said, "Take care of my sheep."

The third time he said to him, "Simon son of John, do you love me?"

Peter was hurt because Jesus asked him the third time, "Do you love me?" He said, "Lord, you know all things; you know that I love you."

Jesus said, "Feed my sheep. Very truly I tell you, when you were younger you dressed yourself and went where you wanted; but when you are old you will stretch out your hands, and someone else will dress you and lead you where you do not want to go." Jesus said this to indicate the kind of death by which Peter would glorify God. Then he said to him, "Follow me!"

Peter turned and saw that the disciple whom Jesus loved was following them. (This was the one who had leaned back against

Jesus at the supper and had said, "Lord, who is going to betray you?") When Peter saw him, he asked, "Lord, what about him?"

Jesus answered, "If I want him to remain alive until I return, what is that to you? You must follow me." Because of this, the rumor spread among the believers that this disciple would not die. But Jesus did not say that he would not die; he only said, "If I want him to remain alive until I return, what is that to you?"

This is the disciple who testifies to these things and who wrote them down. We know that his testimony is true.

Then the eleven disciples went to Galilee, to the mountain where Jesus had told them to go. When they saw him, they worshiped him; but some doubted.

Then Jesus came to them and said, "All authority in heaven and on earth has been given to me. Therefore go and make disciples of all nations, baptizing them in the name of the Father and of the Son and of the Holy Spirit, and teaching them to obey everything I have commanded you. And surely I am with you always, to the very end of the age."

On one occasion, while he was eating with them, he gave them this command: "Do not leave Jerusalem, but wait for the gift I am going to send you which my Father has promised, and which you have heard me speak about. For John baptized with water, but in a few days you will be baptized with the Holy Spirit. But stay in the city until you have been clothed with power from on high."

So when the Lord Jesus had led them out to the vicinity of Bethany, they met together, and they asked him, "Lord, are you at this time going to restore the kingdom to Israel?"

He said to them: "It is not for you to know the times or dates the Father has set by his own authority. But you will receive power when the Holy Spirit comes on you; and you will be my witnesses in Jerusalem, and in all Judea and Samaria, and to the ends of the earth."

After he had said this, he lifted up his hands and blessed them. While he was blessing them, he left them and was taken up into heaven before their very eyes, and a cloud hid him from their sight. And he sat at the right hand of God.

They were looking intently up into the sky as he was going, when suddenly two men dressed in white stood beside them. "Men of Galilee," they said, "why do you stand here looking into the sky?

This same Jesus, who has been taken from you into heaven, will come back in the same way you have seen him go into heaven."

Then the apostles worshiped him. And they returned to Jerusalem with great joy from the hill called the Mount of Olives, a Sabbath day's walk from the city.

When they arrived, they went upstairs to the room where they were staying. Those present were Peter, John, James and Andrew; Philip and Thomas, Bartholomew and Matthew; James son of Alphaeus and Simon the Zealot, and Judas son of James.

They all joined together constantly in prayer, along with the women and Mary the mother of Jesus, and with his brothers. And they were continually at the temple, praising God.

Jesus took his earthly body with him rather than leave it behind as if it were unworthy of his divinity. He raised our human flesh with him into the heavens, even to the right hand of God—even to being God. But this body made of dust was forever transformed by his suffering and resurrection. Through the incarnation Jesus humbled and emptied himself to become like us; now, in his ascension, he allows us to share in his divinity and opens up a way for us into heaven.

✠ EPHESIANS 1:17–23

I keep asking that the God of our Lord Jesus Christ, the glorious Father, may give you the Spirit of wisdom and revelation, so that you may know him better. I pray that the eyes of your heart may be enlightened in order that you may know the hope to which he has called you, the riches of his glorious inheritance in his people, and his incomparably great power for us who believe. That power is the same as the mighty strength he exerted when he raised Christ from the dead and seated him at his right hand in the heavenly realms, far above all rule and authority, power and dominion, and every name that can be invoked, not only in the present age but also in the one to come. And God placed all things under his feet and appointed him to be head over everything for the church, which is his body, the fullness of him who fills everything in every way.

ANCIENT WISDOM FROM AUGUSTINE OF HIPPO

Today our Lord Jesus Christ ascended into heaven; let our hearts ascend with him. Listen to the words of the Apostle: *If you have risen with Christ, set your hearts on the things that are above where Christ is, seated at the right hand of God; seek the things that are above, not the things that are on earth.* For just as he remained with us even after his ascension, so we too are already in heaven with him, even though what is promised us has not yet been fulfilled in our bodies.

Christ is now exalted above the heavens, but he still suffers on earth all the pain that we, the members of his body, have to bear. He showed this when he cried out from above: *Saul, Saul, why do you persecute me?* And when he said: *I was hungry and you gave me food.*

Why do we on earth not strive to find rest with him, in heaven even now, through the faith, hope and love that unites us to him? While in heaven he is also with us; and we while on earth are with him....He is the Son of Man by his union with us, and we by our union with him are children of God.

Hear our prayers, O Lord, and, as we confess that Christ, the Savior of the world, lives with you in glory, grant that, as he himself has promised, we may perceive him present among us also, to the end of the ages; who lives and reigns with you and the Holy Spirit, one God, for ever and ever. Amen.

CHAPTER TWELVE

The Day of Pentecost

The women and men who had followed Jesus are gathered once again in the upper room on a warm Sunday morning. Ten days ago Jesus had told the disciples that they would receive a gift from above, but they weren't sure what to expect. Early in his ministry Jesus had told Nicodemus, a Pharisee whom he loved and befriended, that the Spirit is like a rushing wind—no one knows where it comes from or where it will go next.

It is Pentecost, the fiftieth and final day of the barley harvest and the beginning of the wheat harvest. This is also the day God gave Moses the Ten Commandments at Mount Sinai. On the fiftieth day after the Israelites left Egypt, God came down with a loud trumpet sound and engulfed Mount Sinai with fire. On the fiftieth day after Christ's resurrection, God will come down upon Mount Zion with a loud, rushing wind and tongues of fire. On the fiftieth day after the exodus from Egypt, God gave his commandments written on tablets of stone. On the fiftieth day of our exile from the slavery of sin, God gives the Spirit, who breathes life into the words of the commandments—a new commandment of love for God and neighbor, written on the tablets of human hearts.

And so the group of men and women who had followed Jesus to the end waited in the space between heaven and earth. When the gift of the Spirit came, the sorrow and grief they had felt at the time of Christ's passion finally melted away into a sea of euphoria. They spilled out into the streets of Jerusalem, staggering drunk with joy.

These were miracle days, when anything was possible.

In my former book, Theophilus, I wrote about all that Jesus began to do and to teach until the day he was taken up to heaven, after giving instructions through the Holy Spirit to the apostles he had chosen.

In those days Peter stood up among the believers (a group numbering about a hundred and twenty) and said, "Brothers and sisters, the Scripture had to be fulfilled in which the Holy Spirit spoke long ago through David concerning Judas, who served as guide for those who arrested Jesus. He was one of our number and shared in our ministry."

(With the reward he got for his wickedness, Judas bought a field; there he fell headlong, his body burst open and all his intestines spilled out. Everyone in Jerusalem heard about this, so they called that field in their language Akeldama, that is, Field of Blood.)

"For," said Peter, "it is written in the Book of Psalms:

"'May his place be deserted;
let there be no one to dwell in it,'

and,

"'May another take his place of leadership.'

"Therefore it is necessary to choose one of the men who have been with us the whole time the Lord Jesus went in and out among us, beginning from John's baptism to the time when Jesus was taken up from us. For one of these must become a witness with us of his resurrection."

So they proposed the names of two men: Joseph called Barsabbas (also known as Justus) and Matthias. Then they prayed, "Lord, you know everyone's heart. Show us which of these two you have chosen to take over this apostolic ministry, which Judas left to go where he belongs." Then they cast lots, and the lot fell to Matthias; so he was added to the eleven apostles.

When the day of Pentecost came, they were all together in one place. Suddenly a sound like the blowing of a violent wind came from heaven and filled the whole house where they were sitting. They saw what seemed to be tongues of fire that separated and came to rest on each of them. All of them were filled with the Holy

Spirit and began to speak in other tongues as the Spirit enabled them.

Now there were staying in Jerusalem God-fearing Jews from every nation under heaven. When they heard this sound, a crowd came together in bewilderment, because each one heard their own language being spoken. Utterly amazed, they asked: "Aren't all these who are speaking Galileans? Then how is it that each of us hears them in our own native language? Parthians, Medes and Elamites; residents of Mesopotamia, Judea and Cappadocia, Pontus and Asia, Phrygia and Pamphylia, Egypt and the parts of Libya near Cyrene; visitors from Rome (both Jews and converts to Judaism); Cretans and Arabs—we hear them declaring the wonders of God in our own tongues!" Amazed and perplexed, they asked one another, "What does this mean?" Some, however, made fun of them and said, "They have had too much wine."

Then Peter stood up with the Eleven, raised his voice and addressed the crowd: "Fellow Jews and all of you who live in Jerusalem, let me explain this to you; listen carefully to what I say. These people are not drunk, as you suppose. It's only nine in the morning! No, this is what was spoken by the prophet Joel:

"'In the last days, God says,
    I will pour out my Spirit on all people.
Your sons and daughters will prophesy,
    your young men will see visions,
    your old men will dream dreams.
Even on my servants, both men and women,
    I will pour out my Spirit in those days,
    and they will prophesy.
I will show wonders in the heavens above
    and signs on the earth below,
    blood and fire and billows of smoke.
The sun will be turned to darkness
    and the moon to blood
    before the coming of the great and glorious
    day of the Lord.
And everyone who calls
    on the name of the Lord will be saved.'

"People of Israel, listen to this: Jesus of Nazareth was a man accredited by God to you by miracles, wonders and signs, which

God did among you through him, as you yourselves know. This man was handed over to you by God's deliberate plan and foreknowledge; and you, with the help of wicked men, put him to death by nailing him to the cross. But God raised him from the dead, freeing him from the agony of death, because it was impossible for death to keep its hold on him. David said about him:

"'I saw the Lord always before me.
Because he is at my right hand,
        I will not be shaken.
Therefore my heart is glad and my tongue rejoices;
        my body also will rest in hope,
because you will not abandon me to the grave,
        you will not let your Holy One see decay.
You have made known to me the paths of life;
        you will fill me with joy in your presence.'

"Brothers and sisters, we all know that the patriarch David died and was buried, and his tomb is here to this day. But he was a prophet and knew that God had promised him on oath that he would place one of his descendants on his throne. Seeing what was ahead, he spoke of the resurrection of the Messiah, that he was not abandoned to the grave, nor did his body see decay. God has raised this Jesus to life, and we are all witnesses of the fact. Exalted to the right hand of God, he has received from the Father the promised Holy Spirit and has poured out what you now see and hear. For David did not ascend to heaven, and yet he said,

"'The Lord said to my Lord:
    "Sit at my right hand
        until I make your enemies
    a footstool for your feet."'

"Therefore let all Israel be assured of this: God has made this Jesus, whom you crucified, both Lord and Messiah."

When the people heard this, they were cut to the heart and said to Peter and the other apostles, "Brothers, what shall we do?"

Peter replied, "Repent and be baptized, every one of you, in the name of Jesus Christ for the forgiveness of your sins. And you will receive the gift of the Holy Spirit. The promise is for you and your children and for all who are far off—for all whom the Lord our God will call."

With many other words he warned them; and he pleaded with them, "Save yourselves from this corrupt generation." Those who accepted his message were baptized, and about three thousand were added to their number that day.

They devoted themselves to the apostles' teaching and to fellowship, to the breaking of bread and to prayer. Everyone was filled with awe at the many wonders and signs performed by the apostles. All the believers were together and had everything in common. They sold property and possessions to give to anyone who had need. Every day they continued to meet together in the temple courts. They broke bread in their homes and ate together with glad and sincere hearts, praising God and enjoying the favor of all the people. And the Lord added to their number daily those who were being saved.

Then the disciples went out and preached everywhere, and the Lord worked with them and confirmed his word by the signs that accompanied it.

In this passage, Paul describes the unity of the scattered children of God in terms of the various parts of the human body working together, each part necessary for its survival. And like one human body, we all breathe one Spirit.

✠ 1 CORINTHIANS 12:3B–7, 12–13

No one can say, "Jesus is Lord," except by the Holy Spirit. There are different kinds of gifts, but the same Spirit distributes them. There are different kinds of service, but the same Lord. There are different kinds of working, but in all of them and in everyone it is the same God at work. Now to each one the manifestation of the Spirit is given for the common good.... Just as a body, though one, has many parts, but all its many parts form one body, so it is with Christ. For we were all baptized by one Spirit so as to form one body—whether Jews or Gentiles, slave or free—and we were all given the one Spirit to drink.

✠ Ancient Wisdom from Irenaeus of Lyons

When the Lord told his disciples *to go and teach all nations* and to *baptize them in the name of the Father and of the Son and of the Holy Spirit,* he conferred on them the power of giving men new life in God.

He had promised through the prophets that in these last days he would pour out his Spirit on his servants and handmaids, and that they would prophesy. So when the Son of God became the Son of Man, the Spirit also descended upon him, becoming accustomed in this way to dwelling with the human race, to living in men and to inhabiting God's creation. The Spirit accomplished the Father's will in men who had grown old in sin, and gave them new life in Christ.

Luke says that the Spirit came down on the disciples at Pentecost, after the Lord's ascension, with power to open the gates of life to all nations and to make known to them the new covenant. So it was that men of every language joined in singing one song of praise to God, and scattered tribes, restored to unity by the Spirit, were offered to the Father as the firstfruits of all the nations.

This was why the Lord had promised to send the Advocate: he was to prepare us as an offering to God. Like dry flour, which cannot become one lump of dough, one loaf of bread, without moisture, we who are many could not become one in Christ Jesus without the water that comes down from heaven. And like parched ground, which yields no harvest unless it receives moisture, we who were once like a waterless tree could never have lived and borne fruit without this abundant rainfall from above. Through the baptism that liberates us from change and decay we have become one in body; through the Spirit we have become one in soul.

O God, you have created all things by the power of your Word, and you renew the earth by your Spirit: Give now the water of life to those who thirst for you, that they may bring forth abundant fruit in your glorious kingdom; through Jesus Christ our Lord. Amen.

✠

Suggestions for Further Reading

Borg, Marcus J., and John Dominic Crossan. *The Last Week*. San Francisco: Harper Collins, 2006.

Brown, Raymond E. *The Death of the Messiah: From Gethsemane to the Grave,* vols. 1 and 2. New York: Doubleday, 1994.

King, Philip J., and Lawrence E. Stager. *Life in Biblical Israel*. Louisville: Westminster John Knox Press, 2001.

Monti, James. *The Week of Salvation: History and Traditions of Holy Week*. Huntington: Our Sunday Visitor Books, 1993.

Sanders, E. P. *The Historical Figure of Jesus*. London: The Penguin Press, 1993.

The Temple Institute: http://www.templeinstitute.org/illustrated_tour.htm

Ward, Benedicta. *In the Company of Christ: A Pilgrimage Through Holy Week*. New York: Church Publishing, 2005.